Design

DESIGN

The University of Massachusetts Press   Amherst, 1979

Purpose,
Form
and
Meaning

John F. Pile

Copyright © 1979 by The University of Massachusetts Press

All rights reserved

Library of Congress Catalog Card Number 78-53182

ISBN 0-87023-257-6

Printed in the United States of America

Library of Congress Cataloging in Publication Data

Pile, John F.

Design.

Bibliography: p.

Includes index.

1. Design.   2.   Communication in design.

I.   Title.

NK1510.P57   745.4   78-53182

ISBN 0-87023-257-6

ACKNOWLEDGMENTS   This book was made possible by a grant for research and writing from the Graham Foundation for Advanced Studies in the Fine Arts for which the author expresses special appreciation.

Editorial assistance by Susan Braybrooke and help with picture research by Elizabeth Grossman were also of significant assistance to the author.

Illustrative material has come from many sources and thanks are offered to the manufacturers and designers who have provided such material. Every effort has been made to credit sources and photographers wherever possible. Many illustrations are from clippings, slides, or other documents in the author's collection and sources have been, in many cases, difficult to trace. A general apology is offered here for any errors or omissions in crediting sources that may have occurred.

Contents

Foreword

THIS BOOK is concerned with questions about how the things that human beings make to aid and modify their lives are formed. My interest in these matters has roots in childhood—the time when we all devote a major part of our time and energy to exploring the world in which we find ourselves. As a city child, the natural world appeared to me as a somewhat exotic background to be visited and admired, but always a trifle remote. Reality, the foreground of my interests, lay in the streets and their buildings, in the boats on the river and the railroad trains that one could watch where main lines passed over bridges, as they cut through parks or stopped in stations.

I suppose it was building models of all these familiar things with blocks that taught me that, unlike natural situations, presented to us as given, these humanly made things are shaped entirely by choice, as a result of human decisions and preferences. We can make the things we make any way we wish, constrained only by natural physical realities. Growing up in Philadelphia in the 1930s, I found that boats and trains and, when I could arrange to see them, airplanes and dirigibles (they still existed then) were real and important for me in a way that the rugs, chairs and lamps in my family's home were not. Some old houses and churches in Philadelphia had a similar fascination for me, but I could find only one new building that seemed to share the same ability to involve me. It was Howe and Lescaze's Philadelphia Saving Fund Society tower, in 1932 the only modern building in Philadelphia or, for that matter, in the whole United States. Otherwise, I found my interests more engaged by the Burlington *Zephyr,* a pioneer streamlined train, the curious (and unpopular) Chrysler "Airflow" automobiles and the buildings of world's fairs in Chicago and New York than by the pseudo-Grecian dignity of our local art museum. Arriving in architectural school in the 1940s, I realized that I had walked into the late phases of a struggle that is still not entirely resolved.

My school had been a leading exponent of the French Beaux-Arts tradition in America, and had trained many of the best-known architects who, in the 1920s and 1930s, settled into a kind of stripped-classical vocabulary that we now associate with WPA-funded post offices and court houses. It was impossible to ignore European developments that had closer ties with my ships, trains and airplanes, but a curious schism existed among our teachers and even, sometimes, within the mind of a single teacher, between the traditional views based in an academic, aesthetic tradition, and the modernist attitudes that had a more mechanistic bent. As students, we came to know about Le Corbusier, Gropius and the Bauhaus, but we were left to debate among ourselves, and occasionally with a tolerant instructor, the merits of the ideas that these people represented. The "old guard" could offer us astonishing techniques for producing results that most of us regarded as absurd, while the new directions were still suspect. It was a time of transition, when neither the old nor the new ways were really established as accepted dogma.

However confusing this may have been to us as students, it led us to ask fundamental questions about the purposes involved in designing anything. There was no doubt that most buildings were not only intended to do a particular job well, but were also expected to be solidly and economically built. But how did one arrive at their form, appearance and whole character? I soon discovered that my instructors had drastically different views about such questions and that, in most cases, they did not really want to waste time with such global issues. As a student, one would do best by learning to draw well, getting good grades in materials and methods and following the advice of design instructors without too many questions.

Graduated from architectural school, I found myself teaching design and, at the same time, working for a succession of practitioners in architecture and industrial design. Quite dogmatic about how they wanted to do things, my employers were even less inclined than my teachers, to discuss the reasons why. My students were possibly even more anxious than I had been to find out why, and this led me to focus on forming reasons. The certainty that comes of minimal knowledge and experience, made me, I suspect, a source of opinionated design doctrine that must have been as frustrating to my students as the vagueness that my teachers had offered me.

I am still, even now, unwilling to slide back into the easy belief that there are no answers to difficult questions. As the problems of designing the elements that make up the modern environment become more and more complex, I cannot imagine that either uncritical acceptance of expanding technology or relaxed acceptance of a random "creativity" are likely to improve the character of the world that we make for ourselves. We need, instead, to relate what we do to some logical framework through which our needs and our wants can be translated into constructed reality by a process that has some logical underpinning, and gives some hope for at least a limited degree of success. In areas where scientific ideas have been brought to bear, we accept the idea that all results have causes, and that desired results can be generated by synthesizing suitable causes. A comparable linkage is available to us in the areas that we label "creative," if we are willing to examine what we really need to achieve and relinquish the inclination to insist on irrationality as a necessary, or even desirable characteristic of work that includes any element of the artistic.

If such ideas were totally new and revolutionary, putting them forward might seem daring and controversial. In fact, these are not new ideas at all. We are surrounded by evidence that objects, buildings, towns and even the total setting of life in times and places that have not been overwhelmed by modern industrial technology have been useful, well made and logically expressive of their time and place—or as we usually express it, aesthetic. It is only in the most developed of so-called civilizations, in the last century and a half, that, while making extraordinary technical progress, we have lost any conception of how to use our skills to put together an acceptable setting for our lives. The logic behind the successes of past and remote design practices is either unformed, unwritten or written in terms that now seem archaic and therefore of only limited help to us. But by examining the evidence of real things and places accessible to us, it is not hard to find consistencies so broad that they suggest a general theory of design, broad enough and logical enough to give us hope that the chaos of the physical circumstances of modern life is neither inevitable nor inescapable.

In trying to develop in work with my students and in writing this book, such a general point of view about the purposes of design, I am reassured to find that I am not being in any way original. The central ideas involved are discoverable in the natural world and are expressed in one way or another in the writing and the work of any number of theorists, critics and practitioners of design. It is a typically modern problem that these logical and, in a way, obvious ideas, have become hard to discover. They have become lost in a confusion of other ill-formed, illogical and contradictory notions, that have equal or greater visibility, and can seem, at least on superficial exposure, equally convincing.

Introduction

I T IS A COMMON, usually critical, observation on life in the modern, technologically developed world to say that it is materialistic. We are a population heavily oriented toward things. We work to produce things and to earn what we need to acquire them for ourselves. We measure individual success largely in terms of things owned—houses, cars, television sets and similar consumer goods. We talk of a standard of living which is measured, in the main, by the per capita count of refrigerators, flush toilets and bathtubs. Scientific and technical achievements often occur as events (a moon landing, for example), yet they are events accomplished with the aid of new and remarkable things such as supersonic aircraft, rockets, orbiting satellites, atomic reactors or, at a different scale, artificial heart valves or kidneys.

The concept of progress in human affairs is, if we are realistic, almost entirely concerned with materialistic, that is to say, technological progress. We describe as primitive any society that exists with a limited inventory of comparatively simple things. When we speak of underdeveloped countries, we mean nations whose per capita count of technically advanced goods is low. The absence of technically advanced equipment of course has consequences for underdeveloped countries. Poor diet, disease and a generally low standard of living are characteristic of underdevelopment but the remedies we know of are, in general, technological. Electric power, gasoline engines, modern hospitals, printed books, radios and television sets are proposed as solutions to world problems by the developed countries that produce them and by the people who lack them.

Historically, the rise of civilization is clearly traceable in these technological terms. If we seek a similar history of progress in other terms, such as humane and intelligent behavior, quality of thought, or artistic achievement, the concept of progress becomes very doubtful. We often pretend that we can trace progress in such terms, but it is difficult to make a strong case for them. The impersonal brutality of modern warfare makes savage war seem almost humane in comparison. Cave art and primitive African art are different from the art of the Renaissance or that of our own time, but it is hard to make a case for a steady line of improvement. The literature of prehistoric Greece, of biblical times or of the Renaissance hold up against the best modern work.

It has become fashionable at the present time to attack technology and the special kind of progress it offers, because the realization that technology does not in itself solve all problems is a comparatively recent one. Proposals for slowing technological advance and even for some partial return to "simpler ways" are now very popular and, in many cases, are probably sound. It is assumed here, however, that we are destined to live in a technically complex world in which things inevitably assume major importance. Even those who urge a return to simpler ways usually invest that simpler world with houses, plumbing, powered machinery, printed books and electronic communication. Such a list is already an inventory of a highly technological society, heavily focused on the apparatus of modern living.

We are concerned here with a peculiar paradox of modern life. While we are object oriented, preoccupied with the production, acquisition and consumption of things, we appear curiously indifferent to the character of those things that mean so much to us. We seem to be utterly uncritical of objects, willing to accept and use things that perform badly, are wasteful of our time, our energy, and our physical resources, that are harmful or dangerous, produce troublesome wastes, are hard to maintain and, when finally discarded, pose burdensome problems of disposal. In spite of our belief that we live in the civilization with the highest level of technical achievement in history, we accept with enthusiasm some of the worst artifacts that humanity has ever endured. Average people, or consumers, obviously do not agree to any significant extent with this negative evaluation. It is natural for most people to assume that the products of modern technology are highly desirable. They make possible a way of life very different from any experienced in the past or in underdeveloped parts of the world today. To suggest that all the advantages of modern technology should be given up would be a message with no chance of acceptance.

The struggle between the old ways, whatever they may have been, and new technology has been going on since the beginning of civilization. Stone axes and grass huts were technological inventions introducing improved ways of life. Apart from political history, with its stories of battles and conquests, the history of increasingly civilized everyday life is simply a history of such inventions. Everyone is aware of the sudden acceleration in invention and technological change within the last century or two. Beginning with the industrial revolution, technological change began to accelerate in a way that now makes it increasingly uncertain whether change is automatically to be considered improvement.

This book is concerned with a conviction that the things which make up the modern, manmade, technological world are in most cases badly designed. ("Things" is used in a broad sense to include everything from the manmodified landscape, the city, town or suburb down to the smallest of everyday objects.) The promise of advantage which inventions offer is, more often than not, reduced to dissatisfaction and distress by a failure in our way of deciding how things shall be made. Our lack of precise language to define these concerns is, in a way, a confirmation of this diagnosis. Everyone understands what an invention is; we all know what it is to make something, but the intermediate steps between invention and the delivery of manufactured products dissolves into a mist of unclarity. The gasoline engine is an invention (or perhaps a group of inventions), but the automobile we see in the showroom is not an invention—we call it a product. How has it come to be made exactly as it is, not larger or smaller, not some other shape or color, a mass of details all chosen for us in some obscure way? What name shall we give to these processes of applied technology that deliver their fruits to us for everyday use? All the words we can suggest are in some way unsatisfactory. Engineering describes the work of the specialists who convert invention to practical, produceable devices. Design describes the processes of selecting shapes, sizes, materials and colors to establish the form of something that is to be made. A major part of the engineers' work is design, yet engineers usually avoid aspects of design that are not primarily technical. In many of the artifacts of modern life, technical aspects of design are important to performance, but not to form. A television set works as it does because of the engineering of its electronic parts, but its shape, size, color and details have little necessary connection with its electronic realities. A telephone instrument works as it does because of a complex system, largely unseen, to which it is connected. The instrument that we use can have an infinite variety of shapes and still serve its technical functions.

A house makes use of many modern technological inventions, materials, products and processes, yet engineering rarely makes any contribution to its general concept, its layout and the details that make it a good or a bad place to live. For the planning of houses there is, of course, a specialized design profession, the profession of architecture. And yet, we notice that only a tiny proportion of all houses are designed by architects. In fact, it is hard to pin down the sources of the design of most houses. Where does the speculative builder get his plans? Who designs the mobile home which is now the form of single-family house produced in greatest quantity? Houses are not, it seems, either engineered or designed in any clear sense. They are put together out of available parts by some rule-of-thumb based on habit and advice that flows through commercial channels.

When we study civilizations of the historic past or remote civilizations in the surviving, nonindustrialized primitive world, we study the artifacts of these peoples, confident that they reveal to us the nature of the lives that they housed and supported. The archeologist, the anthropologist and the historian are experts in focusing on this kind of evidence and extracting information from it. If we try to view our own civilization in this way, detaching ourselves from our inevitable involvement with it, it emerges as chaotic and illogical to a degree that must surely be unequaled anywhere else or at any other time in history. It is possible, of course, and currently very fashionable to draw from this situation some grand pessimism. If our civilization is, actually, a final phase of human decline, destined to lead in the near future to the end of human life, it is not inappropriate that evidences of decadence and chaos should be around us in constantly increasing magnitude.

It is also possible to view these matters in a way that is less grandly apocalyptic. It is possible to study the illogical and disturbing aspects of the physical realities of our civilization at a more modest, and possibly more productive level, by putting aside questions of destiny; by avoiding optimism based on no firm evidence, or pessimism generated by extrapolation from the worst that we can observe. Instead, we can look at the realities of our own time in the same way that we study the civilizations of history or the few extant primitive civilizations. This means asking why. Why do we arrange things as we do? What is right about the way we do things, and where are our mistakes? Is it possible to find a way to make the physical realities of our own civilization more rational and responsive to our needs and intentions?

In order to face such questions with any seriousness, it is necessary to trace our way back to some fundamental questions—questions which, like most basic questions, are rarely asked and which, when asked, are possibly a source of irritation. We need to ask, for example, why the physical realities of our environment should matter to us. It is clear that they matter very little to many people (once certain basic minimal standards are achieved). It is a common observation that great thinkers, philosophers, scientists, writers or musicians are often content to live in the most commonplace or even squalid circumstances. Visual artists, in contrast, probably because sensitivity to the environment is a necessary aspect of their work, usually contrive to make their living circumstances both practical and visually coherent, even when this must be achieved against economic and circumstantial odds. The majority of us stand somewhere between these extremes—able to survive and live with some effectiveness despite the bad elements of our environmental surroundings, but still prepared to benefit from whatever may be good. We lead lives that are partly inward, personal and independent of life circumstances, but which are also partly located in time and place and, to that extent, largely a product of the real situations in which we find ourselves.

The realities of *things* are important to all of us. Whether this importance is ultimately favorable or unfavorable to our life experience depends very much on the qualities of the things themselves. An attempt to identify the elements that make up human life experience may be useful at this point. After a little thought, one can sort out two main kinds of experience: the first can be characterized as "interpersonal," that is, relationships with parents, siblings, friends, lovers, enemies, fellow workers, children—even people we have never met, such as politicians, actors or artists with whom we feel a kind of once-removed personal contact via an intermediate device such as a printed publication, radio, cinema or television. These devices lead us into the other aspect of life experience—that of things, not people. We all think of ourselves as having connections with this kind of reality which begin with our sense of birthplace, national identification and residence. Some of these things are less powerful and less oppressive in modern life than they once were, but they are still strong influences. We know that the place where we live is an important factor in shaping our daily life. Even a philosopher or poet, whose mind is centered on inner thinking, will lead a very different life in Paris than in New York, in an African village or on a farm in the United States middle west. Life is different in a city apartment, in a suburban house, in a trailer and in a tent. The experience of travel depends very much on whether it is undertaken by car, train, airplane or ship. The nature of work is very different in an office, in a factory and on a farm not only in the quality of the work itself but also as a result of different tools, equipment and work environment.

The human life setting is made up of components of two kinds—the natural and the humanly created. The larger setting, the universe, the solar system, the earth itself are all natural and fundamentally dominant, since they establish the conditions within which human activity takes place. Until recent times, most human life was dominated by the natural environment. The life of the hunter, the nomad, the farmer or the sailor was a life lived largely in an unmodified, natural out-of-doors in which humanly made artifacts, tents, huts, implements, weapons, and open boats made rather minor modifications. It is only within the last four or five thousand years, with the coming of agriculture, towns and cities, that this situation has gradually changed. It is only within the last two hundred years that this change has accelerated to a degree that has made modern human experience primarily an experience of humanly made places and things.

We do not have an ideal word for the processes of choice and decision-making that determine how *things* are to be made. "Design" will have to serve us, although its many meanings—from "decorative pattern," to the selection of sizes for plumbing pipes—can be a source of confusion. The word is used here to mean the making of decisions about size, shape, arrangement, material, fabrication technique, color and finish that establish how an object is to be made. The object can be a city or town, a building, a vehicle, a tool or any other object, a book, an advertisement or a stage set. Designers are people who make such decisions, although they will, most often, have some other name describing their specialized concern: architect, engineer, town planner or, possibly, craftsman.

In spite of the overwhelming influence that the processes of design—the work of designers—has on modern life, these people and the work they do is very little thought about or discussed in our society. Most people have no idea who designed the house they live in, the building they work in, the automobile they drive or the chair they sit in. They are quite content to enjoy these conveniences to whatever extent possible, to complain occasionally about obvious shortcomings, but to remain in total ignorance about their origins. Ask the average citizen to list the names of some well-known town planners, architects and industrial designers and expect a list of something between two names and none at all.

It is the purpose of this book to make a critical study of this wide range of modern design activity and to try to identify those design directions that are constructive and those that are, on balance, harmful to the realistic purposes of human life. In doing this we will be forced to face one more issue: the issue of the relation of design to art. The design professions are strangely divided on this matter. Engineering and the other strongly technological types of design activity, tend to pull away from any identification with the arts. Architecture has traditionally called itself "the mother of the arts" and is adamant in asserting its right to be included along with painting and sculpture (and, possibly, music) as a primary art. The role of art in modern life is strangely ambiguous: supported, valued and rewarded at times in a way that has almost no precedent, but at the same time suspect and placed in a special category remote from everyday life and so, in a way, from reality. Design is the activity which forms a major part of reality as we experience it. In a technological society, its technological aspects are inevitable.

The degree to which we accept the notion of design as art, and our understanding of the nature of art and its role in our lives, is a key factor in the reality of the modern life experience.

The Scope
of the
Problem
2

$\mathbf{A}$LTHOUGH in recent years a widespread dissatisfaction with the physical realities of modern, technological civilization has developed, it is somewhat unusual to relate this dissatisfaction to criticism of contemporary design. We tend to assume that the *things* which characterize our civilization are as they are because of inevitable pressures of economic, social and political forces and our limited ability, at the current level of scientific progress, to achieve all the things we may desire. While all these are real pressures and factors in shaping how things must be made, they remain only *factors* that interact with one another, but still leave open a vast range of decision-making on which we can exercise our individual judgment. Where a very demanding level of technical performance is required of an object, it is easy to assume that there will be little room for exercise of such judgment, but this is not really so. Consider, for example, the design of an airplane. In order for it to fly at all, it must take certain special shapes that have been found workable for this highly demanding purpose. If it is also to be safe, useful and economically efficient, its designers must be even more narrowly constrained. And yet, aircraft are built in a great variety of configurations, with wings high or low, straight or swept back and with engines in various numbers and placements.

If such demanding performance standards can be realized in such a variety of forms, it is no surprise that most objects have an almost limitless range of possible shapes and sizes. A chair can be of many differing materials, degrees of comfort, sizes or shapes and still be useful. It is this possibility of infinite variety that leads to our confusion about how things should be. We take for granted the luxury of apparently limitless choice in almost everything. Any department store or mail-order

9

catalog offers us furniture, dishes, glassware, apparel and endless appliances and gadgets, each in many differing versions. More often than not, however, the choices are between equally unsatisfactory alternatives. Instead of being able to select the best of a number of excellent things, we must settle for the least bad of a bad lot. If we are searching for things of a strictly utilitarian nature, the situation is not quite as bad as this description suggests. It is easier to locate a well-designed tool, tractor, pump or microscope than it is to find an acceptable armchair, television set, family car or suburban house. In fact, it is in the category of consumer goods that modern industrial production offers us the worst it can achieve. It would be reasonable to expect a materialistic and object-oriented society to develop the finest objects that available technology is capable of producing. The fact that our society does the reverse, suggests that we are suffering from some kind of basic misunderstanding about how things should be designed.

This is, in fact, exactly our situation. We have lost sight of what it is that makes an object truly satisfactory and have substituted a number of absurd beliefs, now so widely accepted that we hardly know we hold them. These misunderstandings about the nature of objects and how they ought to be designed are not only commonplace among the consuming public, but have entered the thinking of design professionals as well, so that even with good intentions, we often achieve design failures or very limited successes. It is possible that the reader may feel that these highly negative assessments of current design achievement are unreasonably pessimistic. It may be appropriate, then, to insert some examples of contemporary reality to make clear the basis for the general indictment of what our society designs and builds. These examples are not chosen to illustrate the worst of what we do; they represent rather the everyday norms that most of us have learned to ignore as a result of the familiarity that numbs our awareness.

1. Arrival in a modern city. The general sense of disorganization results from the unrelatedness of the many elements. The individual elements also—if viewed separately—turn out in most cases to be ill-conceived.

2. A suburb. Land is subdivided to maximize profit for the developer and without regard for its usefulness to the permanent homeowners. Road layout is planned for economy of construction, not for safety or convenience. Houses are oriented along roads, not for view, solar advantage or other climatic considerations. The land is leveled and all trees are cut for convenience in building, leaving the site devastated for a period of many years thereafter.

The chaos typical of the modern fringe.

The suburb. Neither city nor country, promising the merits of both, but delivering only the least desirable aspects of each.

"Ideal" table setting from a homemaking magazine.

The surburban house.

A "recliner"; comfort of a sort regardless of all other values.

3. A suburban house. The plan layout concentrates on formal "showplace" rooms (parlor, dining room) which are rarely used, and treats kitchen and family room, the spaces constantly used, as secondary. Windows are small and scattered with no thought for desirable orientation or view. Design is regarded as an afterthought, involving the addition of a plethora of accessories (railings, dormers, odd windows, patios) and a muddle of varied materials applied to surfaces without logical reason. Gadgets are offered in place of genuine utility (dishwasher, garbage disposal, nooks) as sales features in an effort to intrigue the potential buyer.

4. A reclining lounge chair. Such chairs, with an ingenious mechanism to offer comfort in a range of reclining positions, have a very real utility. The appearance is, in most cases, an effort to disguise the real size, shape and operational modes of the chair with an overlay of decorative detail, intended to suggest some past or remote period that the owner is expected to find artistic. Colonial or Mediterranean details, having little relation to any actual historic or regional realities, are mass produced in a factory along with the mechanism.

5. Table setting. Linen, dishes, silver and glassware are all a mass of small-scale decoration (usually with floral origins) so that no plain surfaces survive anywhere. A curious kind of dappled camouflage results in which people, the food being served, and the articles that make up the setting are all confused into a random pattern of spotty color and form. Taken individually, the items seem to be decorated to suggest times, places or situations in which wealth and elegance were displayed through elaboration. The intention is to support a half-hearted snobbery in which the outpouring of detail will express aspirations to culture, wealth and taste. In reality, the clutter of factory-made banality becomes expressive of emptiness and boredom. The elements intended to synthesize cheerfulness and well-being instead suggest depression and desperation.

6. A modern automobile. It is, perhaps, beating a dead horse to attack the automobile—the American Detroit product in particular. It is so often stated, however, that the worst absurdities of car design are things of the past, that it seems necessary to provide a reminder that we have not by any means reached sanity in this area. The car illustrated is, of course, oversized for its carrying capacity, greedy of increasingly scarce fossil fuel, a source of air pollution in spite of the costly and troublesome emission control devices added to it as afterthoughts, only under pressure of legal requirements. In spite of its legislated safety fea-

The modern automobile.

tures it remains dangerously overpowered, difficult to control and short of such simple safety elements as clear vision through nondistorting glass and truly effective bumper protection. The obvious design features such as the spare-tire shape of the trunk lid (which does not house a tire) and the "opera windows" that offer no vision, characterize the role of the car as an absurd gesture in self-expression—self-expression which is artificially mass-produced and which offers, in the end, only an expression of wastefulness and inanity.

It might seem that these examples have been carefully chosen to put the worst possible face on modern design practice. No doubt it would be possible to find better examples to match each of these distressing ones, but it would not be easy. It would take a careful search, and advance knowledge of where to look. The examples offered really do represent the norms of our civilization; better examples would represent the exceptional or the remarkable, not the familiar.

We must now suspend our critical attack in order to look beyond these routine realities and ask what patterns of thinking stand behind them. Each bad situation has been created with deliberate effort and at considerable cost and has come to be acceptable to the vast majority of people. The ideas they express have pulled away from rationality, but if they are brought out and examined they will be found unacceptable. Such ideas are expressed every day, not only by average people, who make no claim to knowledge of design matters, but also by trained professional designers and the clients and corporate executives who employ them. It is worthwhile listing some of these ideas in order to explore the reasons for rejecting them.

Probably the most frequently expressed of these ideas is the assertion that all design issues are matters of taste and not, therefore, subject to any rational evaluation. We take it for granted that preferences in ice cream flavors, for example, are merely whims that every individual has a right to humor. The popular analogy maintains that a desire for a colonial television console, a house of imitation stone or a tail-finned automobile are no different from a liking for strawberry ice cream. But while all ice cream flavors are (we would like to hope) equally innocuous to human well-being and differ only in incidentals that cannot be evaluated in any logical way, differences in the design of objects are not usually so superficial. If the comparison is shifted to other creative activities such as literature or music, we are led to different conclusions. Whether to read comic books or serious novels, whether to listen to Gregorian chant, Beethoven symphonies or cocktail music is, of course, a matter of taste. No one in our present culture would suggest legislative control in these matters, but no one would suggest that these alternatives are all of equal merit. We know that there is good music and bad, good writing and bad. If we choose the bad knowingly, we have only ourselves to blame. The confusion we must avoid is that of thinking that in design matters there is no good and bad.

If design choices were strictly personal matters (as is the choice of listening or of reading materials) we could accept the idea that there is good and bad, but that the choice itself is a matter concerning only the individual. But most design choices are not so solitary in their impact. To some extent we impose all our design choices on everyone else who comes in contact with them. The decoration of a room is seen by family, friends, or anyone who enters it. The exterior of a house is visible to everyone who passes it and, in the aggregate, becomes the quality of a neighborhood or a city. These are matters that influence a whole population and persist into an extended future.

It must also be remembered that many design decisions, including most of the large ones, are not made by individual users. It is the supermarket owner who decides what the supermarket will be like (with the help of his architect, perhaps, if he retains one to make such decisions); the shopper is exposed to whatever is there unless his dissatisfactions reach a level that leads him to shop elsewhere. The traveler must use the airport the city has built and ride in the airplane the airline provides. An automobile buyer has a range of choice, but a comparatively narrow one among the handful of types in production at a given moment. The analogy with literature and music comes to mind again; we can choose what we like best from what is offered to us, but we have no way of knowing what better things might be, but are not offered us. Publishers of literature, music and recordings offer, it would seem, a wider range of choice and better representation of the best, than do the builders of supermarkets or of automobiles.

The belief that all design preferences are merely matters of taste has close ties with another questionable notion: the view which suggests that whatever most people want should be most available and should be the standard for everything intended for public use. This is an idea that has a kind of superficial appeal in a democratic and commercial society. We elect to office the man who gets the most votes. If we make and build what so many people seem to like, we will be equally democratic in this matter, while also expecting to sell a maximum of whatever it is that we make. "You can't force good things on people if they like bad things," this view runs, and becomes most believable when expressed in the phrase "people get about what they deserve"—in politics and in products alike. The problem here—as in the philosophy, "it's all a matter of taste,"—is that these views side-step the issue that things can be better or worse and say, in effect, that worse is no worse than better— surely a paradox that cannot be seriously accepted. The idea that popular vote can be counted on to seek out the best is not one that is very easy to defend, even in the modern political field. To propose it as a serious test of excellence in creative, artistic and design fields is an absurdity. This view implies the insistence that taped background music is superior to Bach and Mozart, that daytime television soap operas are superior to Shakespeare, and that factory-processed fast-foods are superior to *haute cuisine*. What is less immediately evident is that the typical modern product, building or town are closely parallel in quality, origins and character to canned music, soap opera and fast-foods. They are all produced to satisfy the lowest common denominator of public preference, based on a cynical view that the worst is always more popular than the best.

The driving idea behind democratic directions in political matters is an idealistic belief that, in the long run, people will select what will be best for them. In contrast, the driving idea behind the seemingly comparable practices in the design of goods is a strictly commercial one: that maximum profits will come from maximum sales and that maximum

16

sales will reward whatever appeals to a maximum number of potential buyers. In its more cynical form it can be stated as "if it sells, it's good," but it can also be somewhat more palatably expressed in such phrases as "we give the public what it wants."

Professional designers, in particular the industrial designers of the 1930s, may have added to the confusion over this issue when they promoted their services by urging that better designed products would sell better (and actually, in some cases, demonstrating that this can be the case). It becomes easy to turn this claim to suggest that whatever sells best must be the best designed. Neither of these views can be supported with any consistency. The sale of anything depends on too many factors to make it possible to isolate the issue of design with any clarity. In a later section of this book, in which individual examples are illustrated and discussed, the reader will find histories of well-designed things that have been spectacular successes, for example, the DC-3 airplane, and well-designed things that have never enjoyed wide acceptance in spite of critical success. The Habitat apartment complex built for Expo '67 in Montreal is an example.

In the end, we must conclude that popularity and commercial success are values quite independent of design excellence, although not totally unrelated. Sound design can be a factor in the popular success of a product under some circumstances but cannot alone insure it. It is impossible to make any serious case for the notion that the most successful things are, for that reason, the best designed.

What might be called the "fallacy of commercialism" discussed above has a curious step-child, an even more cynical belief that proposes that only really bad design can be really successful. The basis for this view is a pessimistic and cynical belief that the majority is always wrong and that the bad always drives out the good. It is not a belief that many designers are willing to express publicly, even though it may exist only slightly below the surface. It is more openly expressed by many entrepreneurs, manufacturers and distributors. It is neatly summarized in the phrase of P. T. Barnum, "No man ever went broke underestimating the taste of the public" and can lead to an effort to arrive at bad design for its own sake. Curiously, in order to follow this line of action, it is necessary to have some clear beliefs about what is good in order to know what is bad. It is this potential, for skilled professional participation in a deliberate effort for all that is worst that is probably unique to the design professions. The profession of medicine, for example, has no parallel; a doctor may be inept but it is unthinkable that he might be retained to achieve the worst possible results. The shops that sell gifts, souvenirs or even lamps and lamp shades are showcases of professional effort dedicated to whatever is worst in design thinking.* Once again, it is the list of excellent designs that have been commercially successful that makes it clear that the decision to produce something inferior is not really based on valid evidence that *only* bad things sell. On the other hand, no one can deny that bad things *do* sell.

There is another group of ideas, somewhat differently focused, but equally a source of confusion to clear thought about design directions. These ideas start with a conviction that design is in some way separate from the physical reality of a thing. Perhaps this is a semantic difficulty—a result of defining design in a way that makes it trivial and incidental. In the Victorian era, what we now call design was often referred to as applied art, a very revealing term suggesting that design is something extra, added to, applied, or stuck on, after the facts have been determined in some other way. Where this idea persists, it is not surprising that the significance of design issues will be devalued. This attitude couples easily with the belief that design issues are "merely matters of taste" and the idea that design success is the result of mysterious, inborn skills. A reasonable person expects to be able to evaluate how things work, how they are made, but how they are *designed* (meaning in this case only how they look) is seen as falling into an area of mystique, or of art, where reason and common sense are felt to be unavailing. It is often said that "one must be born with talent" and this notion appeals equally to the person who wants to escape concern with such matters by claiming a lack of such talent himself, and to the person who wants to assert superiority through a claim to unique skills that are not subject to any reasonable evaluation. There can be no denial that people are born with varying inherited characteristics, levels and kinds of intelligence, and special physical abilities, but it is also probable that a very large part of what is called inborn talent is actually learned, perhaps very early and in very subtle ways from the upbringing provided by parents, teachers and the whole range of cultural and environmental circumstances. It is not appropriate here to attempt to explore this complex issue, particularly since the facts about what is inherited and what is culturally determined are still under scientific investigation.

What must be made clear is that, whatever the sources of artistic and

*This is not intended to refer, primarily, to the kind of design referred to as "camp" or "kitsch" in which the willfully unattractive and tasteless is deliberately cultivated as a kind of satire or parody—a form of antiart or antidesign.

design skill, these need not be considerations outside the concern of average people. If one understands the word design to include *all* the decisions about how things will be made and work, as well as the decisions—quite inseparable from these—about how the end product will look, it becomes impossible to shrug off design issues as a minor aspect of reality, of concern only to a special group of aesthetes.

Special groups of self-appointed aesthetes always stand ready to accept the role of arbiters of public taste. Among this group there is still another set of questionable attitudes that has its own supporters.

It is the group of theories that suggest that there are rules, as solid and effective as the laws of nature, governing all aesthetic matters and can be applied to the problem of making objects beautiful. The rule-makers incline toward discussion of some concepts which have their own validity and use, such as the notions of balance, symmetry, proportion and similar abstractions—all terms useful enough in analyzing the visible forms of natural and manmade things—but they suggest that within these concepts it is possible to identify clear laws of what is right and what is wrong. The difficulty that always arises is that these clear laws never emerge in any intelligible form. "Good proportions," we are told, are essential to all aesthetic success, but on closer examination, it turns out that good proportions are an entirely relative and variable matter, recognizable only by the exercise of a special kind of taste, possessed, of course, by the theorist proposing this idea, but not available in any explicable way to others.

Experimental aesthetics, a legitimate branch of psychology, has been searching for clear principles in this area for many years, but the results of its studies do not seem to bring forth any rules of a clear and usable sort. Efforts to discover an ideally proportioned rectangle, for example, tend to arrive at something between a square and a long thin bar. Searches for the most favored color become lost in variable results, depending on the design of the experiment conducted. In the end, context is so powerful a determinant of appropriateness that efforts to locate simple aesthetic rules dissolve in the confusion generated in efforts to extract single variables suitable for orderly experimental study. There have been, and still are systems for establishing mathematical relationships of dimension and shape that are not so simplistic. These extend from the geometric systems devised in ancient Egyptian architecture through the ancient Greek devotion to the golden section* and the Re-

*The golden section, sometimes designated by the Greek letter psi, is the ratio that results when a line is divided so that the short segment has the same relation to the long that the long has to the sum of the two. It works out to be the unique proportion 1:1.618,033 . . .

naissance investigations of typical human body proportions, to such modern schemes as Le Corbusier's "Modulor." All of these systems turn out to be complex and subtle ways of relating elements of dimension in ways that are infinitely varied and adaptable—in no way "rules" that can be easily learned and rigidly applied so as to bring about assured success. Knowledge of the physical principles that stand behind the mechanics of structure, the dynamics of motion, the nature of light and color and all other similar realities are infinitely useful in determining how things can best be formed, but this kind of knowledge is always supportive, never controlling in determining how things can best be done.

When spelled out on paper, none of these views may seem particularly convincing or persuasive, and yet, one or another, or some combination, summarizes the most commonly held attitudes toward design. This is not only the case with laypersons, but also true of design professionals and their influential clients and employers. The poor quality of the design achievement of our era does not come from technical ineptitude, but from misdirection resulting from a loss of clear vision about the purposes of design activities. In primitive and historical societies, these purposes seem to have been intuitively grasped and universally understood, even if rarely and only partially stated. In our own time, the real purposes of design seem to have been lost behind the superficial and illogical views reviewed above. A search for real purpose can best begin by focusing on aspects of society in which design excellence is commonplace, the norm or almost universal. Three such areas—*nature, vernacular design,* and *technological design*—come to mind, and each deserves a fairly detailed examination. The first term hardly needs explanation, but the other two terms need explanation and definition, which is attempted at the beginning of the respective sections.

Nature

THE MOST overwhelmingly effective system of which we have any knowledge is the total system of nature, of which we human beings are a part. When we speak of nature, we are referring to almost everything we know of the universe, except for that very tiny part which is under conscious human control. It is a curious fact of contemporary life that in spite of the broad sweep of nature, only a small part of our experience can be said to be natural, the rest being experience of life circumstances that are of our own deliberate making. Oddly, we admire and accept the natural setting of life, but, very rightly, criticize and worry about the aspects of our environment that we ourselves control.

It is a fairly universal experience to admire and enjoy nature. At every level of civilization, every level of intelligence, in almost every life style, people enjoy going out-of-doors, escaping from cities and buildings and having some direct experience of the natural world as it was before human modifications became so obtrusive. Although the level of interest and knowledge may vary, everyone seems to be able to enjoy the sky, trees, birds and animals. A vacation in the country, a sea voyage, even a visit to the zoo or aquarium are expressions of this universal sense which must derive from a very deep awareness that when we turn our attention to natural things, we are exposing ourselves to the most meaningful levels of reality. Science, the basis of modern life, is simply an organized way of studying the natural world, discovering its principles and making the results available for use in changing our lives as we may wish.

The evolutionary processes which have brought humanity into existence, and the ongoing processes of human life are natural. Until a few thousand years ago, human life was conducted in a natural world with a

minimum of human modification. Even in our highly artificial, modern technological life, these artificial realities are based on aspects of nature. All materials are, in a fundamental sense, natural. Even the most synthetic are synthesized from chemicals or molecules that have their origins in the natural elements. We think of wood as a natural material, metals as technological and therefore in some way less natural, and plastics as totally artificial—and yet in another sense all are essentially natural. A tree, a log, a board and a sheet of plywood represent differing stages in the increasingly complex processing of a natural material. Aluminum or stainless steel are processed forms of natural ores, and plastics are processed forms of petroleum derivatives and other chemicals whose ultimate sources must be in earth, air or water. The processing of raw materials, and the forms into which these materials are worked to become usable objects, are all under the ultimate control of natural laws. The realities of atomic structure, gravity and the laws of physics are natural and *must* be used, never defied, in the efforts of human beings to make the things they need and want.

Design, even of the most artificial of things, is, therefore, firmly based in nature. Design successes can be thought of as indications of a successful relationship with natural elements, and failures as the result of inadvertent, ignorant or willful neglect of this relationship. It is also interesting to consider the way in which these ties with natural phenomena relate to the human aesthetic sense. The almost universal sense that natural things are beautiful and satisfying seems to be suspended only in the rather limited instances where some element of fear enters into the relationship. When someone speaks of "an ugly black thunder cloud," the ugliness sensed is probably an expression of fear that the cloud represents the threat of an unpleasant or dangerous storm. Many people speak of snakes or spiders as ugly, but this seems to be another expression of fear of danger. If those fears can be put aside, thunder clouds, and even poisonous snakes and insects, can be recognized as no less beautiful than any other aspect of nature.

It seems reasonable to speculate that in the 1.3 million years that human life is said to have existed as a natural process within a totally natural environment, a relationship with, and comprehension of, nature has been built up that is not likely to break down within a few thousand years of modern technology. Biological evolution has developed the human animal to operate within nature. The senses and the mechanics of the body relate the human animal to the natural environment, not to an artificial one. As we turn our environment into an artificial one, it is hardly surprising that our success can be measured by the degree to which our artificial efforts can be made to adapt to the senses and physical realities of the naturally developed human animal. When we achieve some degree of success in this regard, the same aesthetic reactions are activated as those triggered by the natural world. We find well-designed objects pleasurable and beautiful, because our biologically established relationship with nature programs our senses and brains to such a positive response.

It is not the intention to suggest here that imitation or reproduction of overtly natural forms is a route to aesthetic success. Printing pictures of flowers on textiles, dishes or papers is not an automatic route to beauty. Organic form (by which we often seem to mean curvilinear form) is not automatically of higher aesthetic value than geometric form. Both exist, of course, in nature. Such simplistic views turn up both in the practice of design and in the literature about it, but only serve to distract from the deeper and more subtle understanding of what it means to parallel nature in principle, without imitating any specific natural forms or processes.

Our relationship with nature is, in a way, a simple and direct version of the developed and systematized process of science. The act of sensing natural things involves an intake of data via the specific senses involved, and the mental result—usually called perception—is the internalizing and grasping of this data. It is the route to understanding what is around us, the ongoing first link in the continuous process of the human being's adaptation to his or her situation in life, through the use of the senses and the mind. By learning through our senses, we become able to think about reality. It is a process that we enjoy and that involves us without any conscious effort on our part. Full understanding involves all the complex tools of modern science and is still probably never totally to be achieved, but understanding at a primary level comes automatically with simple exposure.

In order to keep this discussion from becoming totally abstract, some illustrative examples are included, arranged in a progressive, if arbitrary, manner.

Out-of-doors, except under certain special circumstances, about half of our field of view is usually filled with sky. Sky is, of course, simply space, but it is not usually empty space. By day, the most common visible forms—apart from the sun—are clouds. The very word cloudy has come to mean vague, but in fact, clouds have shape, color and quite specific typical forms that have been named by meteorologists. Alto-

Anvil-shaped thunderhead cloud formation.

Cumulus clouds.

stratus clouds, the feared anvil-top thunderhead form, are highly recognizable and totally different from the typically round and puffy cumulus cloud. When we bother to notice them, these and the other cloud types have aesthetic quality in one way or another, and have always been the delight of landscape painters.

By night, when the sky is clear, we have a view of the varied objects of outer space. The Milky Way, we are told, is an edge view of our universe (our nebula) seen from within. Other complete nebulae are visible to us from our remote viewpoint, but most appear to be mere points of light until enlarged with telescopes. Then they become awesome and spectacular images. Our viewpoint makes of the night sky a random pattern, but it is interesting to notice that we do not find that randomness disturbing—no one complains that the sky is untidy or disorganized. Our need to find pattern has, however, led us to note groupings that are easy to remember, and give them the fanciful names (Orion, Cassiopeia's Chair, Big Dipper) that do not, of course, refer to any physical reality. The realities studied by astronomers are more abstract and complex, and become accessible to vision only through charts and diagrams, which can also be spectacularly beautiful.

The eye and telescope together can put us in touch with such extraordinary images as the planet Saturn, or with the moon's surface, while the new space technology has now made available to us images of our own planet from distances great enough to give us a total view. Close-up views at a scale showing us continents and parts of continents have a special fascination because of the way in which they parallel (and differ from) the various kinds of maps that until recently had been our only means of visual understanding of the earth's geography. Our ordinary contact with the earth's surface is simply our view of landscape (or seascape) and in its visual aspect seems to be an almost universal source of pleasure. Travelers will stop to admire and photograph any place with a good open sweep of view, and will make special trips to unusual locations, such as mountain tops or high towers, to obtain a good view.

Landscape is actually a rather complex visual image, since it is made up of sky, earth's surface and, in most cases, phenomena that have developed on the earth's surface such as wave forms, ice forms, plant growth and, to a lesser degree, traces of animal life. Even the inanimate parts of landscape offer a vast range of complex imagery which can be explored in stages of increasing closeness. The forms of mountains, dunes, rocks, pebbles, grains of sand, mineral crystals and, with suitable magnification, even molecular structure are all available for study and appreciation through visual experience.

The "coal sack" in the southern Milky Way.

Spiral galaxy M-51.

Saturn.

Planet Earth.

Clouds in a landscape.

Alpine landscape. *Landscape with human intervention.*

From the range of natural situations mentioned thus far, it is interesting to consider the kinds of visual satisfactions they evoke in relation to various aesthetic theories. Such concepts as balance, symmetry, pattern, systematic proportion or geometric form show up in nature in only very limited ways and in special circumstances. One might say that randomness comes closer to being a description of these aspects of nature and yet we grasp and understand that what appears as irregular and complex is not really random. It is rather that we have visual access to realities too varied and too subtle to be limited by the kind of shallow conceptualizing that is involved in simplistic aesthetic theory.

What we are really exposed to when we look at natural things is a visible output generated by ongoing processes. In inanimate nature, most of these processes are so slow as to give us an illusion of permanence. The stars seem fixed in place (although astronomers tell us they are moving at staggering rates of speed); the earth's form seems ageless (in spite of volcanos and earthquakes); and we think of mountains as fixed. Solar, lunar and planetary movements are a more visible expression of active process, which relate to weather, tides and seasonal change. On reflection, it is obvious that landscape is subject to constant variation according to time of day, weather and season. How anything appears to be at a particular moment is always—like a still taken from a moving picture—a specially time-fixed view of what is actually a matter of constant change. If this is true of inanimate nature, it is much more strongly true of those processes of life which take place within a time scale that make us poignantly aware of their transitory nature.

Rock surface formations.

For many people, certain aspects of plant life, flowers or trees, have come to represent the *most* beautiful of all things, and this can turn some of our thinking about aesthetics into clichés. Imitation of plant forms (or mere illustration of the forms in surface decoration) can become empty and meaningless through excessive repetition. More thoughtful observation of biological processes tends to discourage simple imitation, but suggests deeper lines of thought about the development of useful form. Just as form can be studied in relation to physical process in inanimate nature, the relation of form to growth becomes the key to the study of living organisms. Living things conduct processes that give them form, sustain their life and bring about the reproduction of the species and it is the close relation between life process, purpose, and structure that brings us close to a direct analogy with human activities in designing and making objects.

It is interesting to notice characteristic ways in which symmetry, so prominent in human design thought, appears in biological form. There are, of course, symmetrical forms in inanimate nature, the near-spherical forms in the rotational bodies and patterns of astronomical systems, and the crystals of materials that we speak of as grown, but random patterns are more common. Clouds, continents and rocks are not symmetrical. In biological processes, symmetry appears as a constantly present formal principle even when it is not evident in casual examination of a particular living thing. A growing plant will often be highly irregular in its total form, but principles of symmetrical growth are still present on closer examination. The simple plants such as molds, mosses and fungi reveal symmetrical form under the microscope, even in those cases where clustered growth appears random to the unaided eye. As fungi become large enough for direct visual examination (mushrooms and toadstools, for example), their symmetrical form becomes evident. It is interesting to notice that the word symmetry brings to mind bilateral symmetry—the familiar symmetry of our own and other animals' bodies—but plant symmetry is often multiaxial or radial. One can cut a mushroom in half along *any* axis and observe a symmetrical cross section.

Plant life also often exhibits (usually in combination with symmetry) spiral patterns and patterns of overlapping spirals. These more complex geometric forms are easily observed in the structure of many flowers. Analysis of these spirals shows that their geometric basis is an almost exact progression of the mathematical progression known as the Fibonacci series of numbers 1, 1, 2, 3, 5, 8, 13 . . . , and so on, in which each number is the sum of the two numbers preceding it.

Applications of the golden section ratio (1:1.618033 . . .) mentioned earlier will generate a spiral based on this same progression. This is an interesting case in which natural form of a kind widely recognized as extraordinarily beautiful, follows mathematical patterns that have been discovered and applied through human invention.

It is also useful to examine biological structure from a functional point of view. A tree, for example, is a living thing carrying on processes that are made possible by its particular form and structure. It is a support structure, which connects roots to leaves, in order to bring nutrients from the ground into position to permit the light of the sun to support the process of photosynthesis. Although all share this general plan, trees vary enormously in the forms characteristic of differing species and in individual form. The differing species represent adaptations to

Giant redwoods.

Bristle-cone pines, among the most ancient of living trees.

Industrial products in decay, and natural processes of decay.

differing climate and other environmental conditions, yet a wide variety can survive with good success in specific locations. Variation among individual trees is a response to even more localized conditions of terrain and weather. Within this range of variation, the consistencies of form and the reliably uniform patterns of individual parts (leaf, flower, seed) form a particularly interesting study in the relationships between uniformity and variation. No two leaves of an oak tree are alike, and yet all share type characteristics that make them readily recognizable as oak leaves. Individual variation disguises the symmetry and order of typical structure, and yet that order is, in some way, observable to us even when individual examples radically depart from it.

Trees deserve special observation for other reasons. Of all living things on earth, they are both the largest and the longest-lived. These two extremes do not, however, characterize the same species. The largest are some of the giant western American trees, such as the well-known sequoias—sometimes as tall as 360 feet—above ground, still larger if the extent of the root structure is taken into account. Although some of these giants are thought to be as old as 4,000 years, the oldest of living things are believed to be bristlecone pines, with living examples estimated to be as old as 4,900 years. Wood survives from dead trees that can be dated back as far as 8,200 years. These are trees of modest size (usually no more than fifty feet in height) that flourish in high, mountainous, almost marginal locations, developing tangled and gnarled forms in some way suggestive of their antiquity and endurance.

One other aspect of plant life that deserves some attention is the pattern of changing forms relating to life cycle (and forms after death as well). Seed, seedling, young plant, mature plant and the no-longer living parts cut from plants or surviving in plant structures after natural death, all seem to share in an order and logic that we find meaningful and visually satisfying. A decaying log or a fallen leaf retain a structure that makes these phases of the process no less real or worthy of study than the mid-lifespan configurations. Manmade things do not always have this characteristic. The products of the most advanced and industrialized production, in particular, typically have only one short moment of ideal form when they are totally fresh and new. Use, age and, particularly damage and decay, tend to make them ugly and useless. An automobile is at its best when it leaves the dealer's showroom and begins from that point onward a decline that ends in the depressing wrecks of a junkyard. The life pattern of a plant, a fruit or vegetable or a tree does not follow such a consistently declining pattern.

Although most plants have some limited ability to move, and some aspects of plant life are highly mobile (wind-blown spores, for example), it is broadly true that plants have a fixed location once established, while animal life is highly mobile. Human beings, now the most mobile of all animals, naturally enough find the other animal species intensely interesting, since they represent alternative forms of a basically similar life. Historically, animals have had enormous importance in human life as threat and enemy, as food source, as power supply, as ally and friend. All of these roles tend to be diminished in modern technological society, particularly urban society, but survive nonetheless, in less visible or less respected forms than in previous eras. In developed countries, animals have largely disappeared as a source of power or transportation, but their importance in food production is, if anything, increased. Their role in myth and religion has been put aside, but they survive in the mind as the symbols of dreams and fantasies to an extent that we tend to underestimate.

We also tend to think of all animal life in terms of a handful of species that are large, dramatic, familiar as domestic pets, or otherwise close to us. It is easy to forget that the numerically dominant forms of animal life are those less obtrusive, subvisible residents of the sea that for various reasons fail as a constant focus of our attention. Only within the last few years have we become aware that our interference with the earth's population of other animals can be hurtful to our human interests. We have discovered that rabbits can be a problem when introduced in a continent (Australia) where they are not subject to natural control, and that in our zeal to eliminate the irritation caused by certain insects, we risk extensive and frightening consequences in the balance of nature on which our habitable environment depends.

Like plant forms, animal forms include a fantastic variety of types and, unlike plant forms, demonstrate mechanisms for locomotion in water, over land and in flight. At the smallest and simplest level, animals are represented by the protozoa. Some 20,000 species have been identified, most of only one cell. To describe the living cell as simple is highly misleading since the study of cell biology is a continuing field of scientific work of great importance. The simplicity of the protozoa is, then, only relative—as compared with the complexities of multicellular life. One is not ordinarily aware of the existence of these animals because (in most cases) they are accessible to vision only through the microscope. It is easy to imagine the amazement van Leeuwenhoek must have felt when his newly developed instrument revealed the astonishing variety of form in life at this scale.

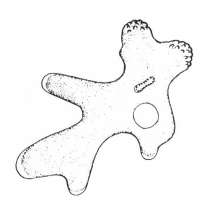

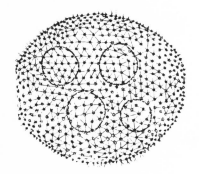

Amoebalike Metachaos discoides, and Volvox aureus colony of 1,000 to 3,000 cells grouped in a hollow ball.

The amoeba has become a type familiar to everyone because of its curiously variable and "unformed" form. Conscious human activity did not uncover it for study as a form until recent times, and it is interesting to speculate whether the awareness gave us the concept of "amoebic form." More consistent and clearly defined form is common to other species, but there is no one "typical" example; indeed the variety seems to equal that of all other living things together. The geometry of structure is especially striking among certain protozoa that form "colonies," or groupings of cells that together take on characteristic form. The well-known, and often illustrated volvox aureus colony is an example in which several thousand cells group together to form a hollow ball as large as one-half millimeter (1/50-inch) in diameter. Spiral forms are also characteristic of some species which exhibit at microscale the kind of form that we associate with many sea and snail shells. Once again the mathematics of the Fibonacci series is found to describe the geometry that emerges.

Insects, at least in the case of the larger species, are readily visible and therefore more widely known. Certain types, such as moths and butterflies are well known for their beauty and attract attention to the

Gonyaulax excavata. Complex geometry of structure at a microlevel accessible only to the scanning electron microscope.

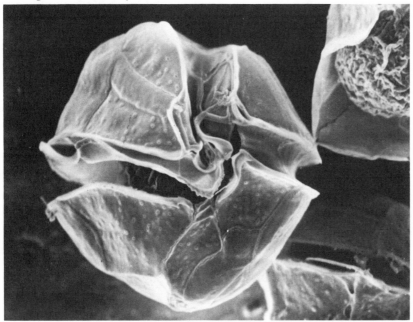

Spiral growth pattern.

significance of their color and surface marking. Color is a characteristic of material arising from the ways in which it reflects or absorbs light. One would expect its incidence to be accidental as it is in inanimate nature. Perhaps this is the role of color in some living things (possibly in man), but in others, natural selection has developed color and color pattern to serve the species in a purposeful way. The purposes are in some cases obscure, but in others can be clearly explained in relation to species or sexual identification, protection through camouflage, or to present a threat to natural enemies. Since many insects are builders of structures, these take on special interest in any study of design in nature. Nests, "hills," hives and webs are often remarkable engineering feats, which in some cases (such as the spider's web), employ very subtle and difficult principles that human engineers have mastered only recently, if at all. And yet, these structures are not planned, designed or engineered in the way humanly developed projects must be. Spiders do not take to a drafting table and, with slide rule and computer, develop plans for their tension structures. Ants do not work from blueprints in order to build hills on the scale of cities, even though this work requires amazingly organized effort on the part of huge teams. The plans and construction methods have instead all been developed by the infinitely slow processes of evolution, and are programmed into the individual insect at birth. The relationship between standardization—the repetition of form in generation after generation of a species—and flexibility to modify and adapt to unique circumstances, is particularly interesting to observe. All the webs of a particular spider are in one sense identical, but in another sense no two are alike.

Fish are better known to us than their underwater habitat might suggest, because their forms are familiar in the market or on the dinner plate. The display of fish in aquariums and their frequent observation in water, with the help of diving and other special gear is another demonstration of a widely felt, tacit admiration for the appearance of these forms of life. The shells of invertebrate fish are interesting examples of structures constructed by living organisms in one sense as part of the living body, but in another sense, separate from it and capable of surviving long after the death of the occupant. Many of these shells again remind us of the Fibonacci series, and the widely felt aesthetic appreciation of these much-collected objects is a reminder of the connection between geometry and the golden section. In section, some of these shells offer startling parallels with mechanical forms developed through human invention.

Spider web.

Warning display in which an undefended moth imitates a more fearsome creature.

Common garden spider with dramatic color marking.

Chambered nautilus shell sectioned to show internal structure.

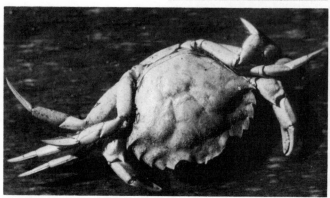

Shell of invertebrate fish.

Spotted file fish.

36

The vertebrate fish bring us a step closer to our own type of bodily organization with flexible skeleton, variety of complex and separable organs and external covering of skin. Reptiles introduce a group to which human observers often bring feelings of fear. (Some reptiles are, indeed, genuinely dangerous, although the fear reaction tends to become exaggerated through ignorance and myth.) Fear is easily converted into the concept of ugliness, yet anyone who has taken the trouble to put aside prejudice, will recognize extraordinary form and structure even among those animals that are genuinely dangerous. The skeletons of many living things are as extraordinary as the complete living animal. Cross sections and diagrams of the subsystems of animal structure (nerves, circulation, reproduction) are also routes to visual contact with the enormous complexity of most living things.

It is probably not necessary to offer much additional comment on the familiar species of birds and mammals since their examination tends to confirm many of the observations already made. Birds are nest builders and their eggs are well known as an aesthetic form of great simplicity and subtlety. Birds and mammals exhibit widely varied external color and marking patterns, usually explainable in terms of species or sex identification or as camouflage.

The issue of symmetry in living things is a rewarding area of observation and study. Bilateral symmetry is characteristic of a very large part of the animal world, but even where it is clearly the dominant principle, it is often modified and varied. Many organs are twinned (eyes, kidneys, feet) while others are single (mouth, spinal column) and located on center. Other single organs (heart, liver) are located off center. External markings are often symmetrical but also often random with respect to the central axis.

Size is another aspect of living animals that can lead to interesting speculation. Each species produces a range of sizes, but a range that has narrow limits. A giant mouse or a tiny elephant are unthinkable. The laws of physics and the presence of gravitational force at the earth's surface have been powerful determinants of animal form and the relation of size to form. As animals become larger, the relation of weight to structural requirements changes. It has been suggested that it would be possible to estimate the size of a previously unknown species from illustrations that offer no evidence of scale, simply by analyzing shape. Sea animals, less dominated by the force of gravity, are consequently less subject to this influence. A whale is quite similar to a polliwog in form. An elephant is very different from a mouse.

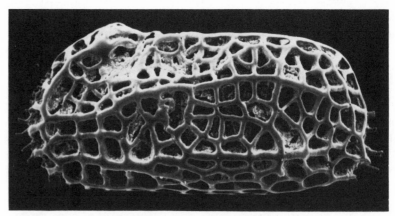

Ostracode skeleton (actual size less than 1 mm. in length).
Thornback ray of symmetrical form but with random marking, and spider with symmetrical structure and marking.

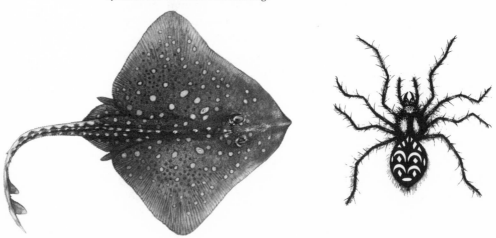

Extremes in size usually limit the survival of a species. Study of prehistoric animals from fossil remains offers some observations on these issues of size. The great dinosaurs, whose sizes continue to overawe us, were successful species for long eras, but environmental changes gradually eroded the advantages of size, leading to their eventual extinction. A possible generalization might be that for any given type, there is a limited range of suitable sizes, a principle that can be observed in many human situations.

The human animal is so familiar to us all as to require no extended comment here. The study of human form has been a major concern of art since its early beginnings and remains essential to all efforts to design objects for human use. Anatomical study by some of the great Renaissance artists did not stop at external surface but penetrated internal structure in a way that we now, unfortunately, consider to be of only specialized medical interest.

If we study nature only in terms of objects mounted as displays, totally dead and devoid of activity, we will severely limit our understanding. Even in the study of static natural objects, we find ourselves forced to recognize process and change. The universe of astronomy and the structure of the atom are equally matters of dynamics. Because change and movement are not as easily reduced to words and pictures as are fixed states, they often tend to drop out of sight. Many modern studies of movement, migrations of species, flight of birds, human muscular actions, wave motion in familiar materials (such as sea waves) or in the less accessible physics of light and other forms of energy are all aspects of form, which, made visible through one or another technique for image creation, become informative, aesthetic and full of suggestion for humanly controlled design activities. Modern physics constantly reminds us that all fixed forms and permanent states are only an illusion. Nothing is exempt from movement in time and space. We only confront slower and faster rates of change.

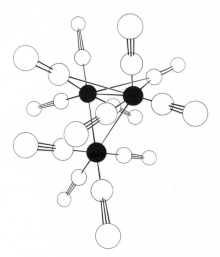

Diagram of chemical molecule made up of a complex grouping of atoms.

Vernacular Design

Following the discussion of so vast a subject as nature, with its unmanageable range of varied forms, it may seem trivial to concern oneself with vernacular design. Indeed, in modern life, the term refers to a comparatively minor aspect of human activity—a backwater and a survival from the past. The term is not widely used or understood, and the examples needed for discussion become more rare every day.

The dictionary defines the word "vernacular" as the common speech, the everyday language; "street Latin" as compared to "book Latin," dialect as compared to educated and standardized language. In his book *Made in America,** John A. Kouwenhoven uses the term and develops the concept extensively, largely in relation to architecture and building, but also as descriptive of other design areas. As might be expected, the term refers to design carried out in an "everyday" or routine way without much conscious thought or formal planning. An analogy might be made with folk music as distinct from composed music, or folk art as different from high art, but this is a slightly misleading comparison. "Folk" in art implies a tradition—most often a peasant tradition—usually strongly involved with a particular, often decorative, style. The term "craft" also comes to mind but, while it relates to, it is not truly descriptive of, vernacular design. Many craftsmen are vernacular designers, but others are quite self-conscious and artful. Many vernacular designs are craft made, but others may be produced in more industrial ways, while still others are so crude as to hardly justify the term craftsmanship.

Design is logically described as vernacular when it does not involve self-conscious development, advance study and planning with models and drawings. It is not the work of trained design experts (although it may involve expert carpenters, masons or other artisans) and it is usually a part of the process of building or making, not a separate operation conducted apart from construction. In a particular area of work, a strong vernacular tradition can often develop which provides answers to questions about how things are to be done. Vernacular tradition usually does not have a very long history or great duration, and is often quite localized, but it relieves the maker of an object of the need to plan ahead and invent ways of doing things—even though there is often great freedom for variety within a particular vernacular tradition.

The reason for making vernacular designs such a strong focus of attention here is that they are often (but by no means always) surprisingly successful both in practical and visual ways. In fact, it is a constant source of surprise and dismay that when replaced by more sophisticated techniques, the vernacular designs often emerge as far superior. As a result, just as nature is a vast source of study and inspiration to designers, vernacular design can, in a much smaller way, demonstrate successful human design efforts. Like design in nature, vernacular design is

*(Doubleday, 1949). Reprinted with the new title *The Arts in Modern American Civilization* (Norton, 1967).

anonymous. In some cases there may be an individual·person responsible for a particular object, but since he is not a trained expert in design, he does not claim credit for what he has done and is usually impossible to seek out. Most often, there is no single individual behind the vernacular object. Instead there is a customary way of doing things, developed over some period of time and accepted as a standard, even though subject to change, adjustment and development. Although this kind of vernacular development is usually rapid—a matter of a few generations at most, it is in some way comparable to the biological process of natural selection. As some familiar object is made over and over again, tiny improvements occur to the makers, and faults or problems are gradually eliminated or at least minimized. The typical vernacular design has thus been refined and developed by many workers, giving it a very thorough shaking out by trial and error. Drastic innovation and radical improvement are not typical of vernacular products; consistency and continuity are. This is probably one of the reasons why sudden efforts to modernize a vernacular product, through a quick revision based on the sophisticated techniques of trained designers, is so often a disappointment.

Every historic era has produced its own vernacular, but it is not possible to attempt a full historic survey here. It is enough to inspect a few examples of nineteenth- and twentieth-century vernacular effort. Except in recently redesigned examples, tools and implements are almost all of vernacular origin. Older tool catalogs provide displays of axes, hammers, squares, levels, saws and planes of marvelously beautiful design. It is not surprising that old tools have become objects for collectors. No one knows who designed these things; they have been made in gradually changing forms for hundreds or thousands of years and their makers have always been concerned with providing functional designs, made from materials that will last. The shapes of heads and handles come to be very delicately adapted to a particular kind of task, and professional users are often very loyal to a particular tool, found to be ideal for a specific job. In recent years, when the amateur or hobbyist has become a prime purchaser of tools, manufacturers have often deviated from the classic vernacular forms in the belief that the uninformed buyer will be attracted more by bright colors or shiny, new-looking materials than by the more solid (and usually more costly) excellence of the vernacular forms. Any serious amateur workman learns to avoid these stylized tools and to prefer the conventional designs.

Household and farm implements follow much the same pattern, al-

Vernacular typography.

Hoe and cultivator—hand powered.

DRYAD HANDICRAFTS . LEICESTER

T30   T32
T31
T50
T42   T51
       T44
       T40
T 94
T176
T175
T 37
T 45
T164   T113   T127   DRYAD

WOODWORK TOOLS

99

Common woodworking tools in a catalog illustration.

Horse-drawn hay rake.

though, in the case of farm equipment, survival is even more threatened by the progress of mechanization that has pushed hand- and horse-powered implements aside. In the case of kitchen and other household products, the threat derives from a combination of advancing mechanization and a more aggressive and sweeping application of the kind of salesmanship that depends on the appearance of newness. Here also, any serious cook knows that chrome trim and streamlined forms are not an assurance of excellence, but on the contrary may be taken as a warning. A wooden spoon, a whisk beater, a knife with a nonstainless steel blade are almost invariably superior to their more stylishly modernized equivalents.

Such household artifacts as dishes, glassware and silver have strong vernacular traditions in the provision of the everyday wares and needs of poorer people. A parallel tradition of richness and elaboration, serving the sophisticated needs of the wealthy, has emphasized the ceremonial, as compared to the ordinary occasion. In recent times, the ease with which such elaboration has been marketed, via industrial production, has caused the demise of vernacular tradition. The cheapest of industrially made dishes, glasses and silver are now simply imitations of the decorated wares of the wealthy of some years ago. There are exceptions, of course, but surviving vernacular designs still in production are becoming increasingly rare. Simple plates, cups and crocks are now usually to be found only in antique shops or as imports from places where vernacular tradition survives (China or France, perhaps, although vernacular products are being pushed aside even in these places). Restaurant wares of the more utilitarian sort preserve some vernacular designs, although the classically familiar French wine glass becomes harder and harder to find, even in France. Examples of vernacular surface decoration appear among some of these things. A bowl with a blue painted fish is a Chinese tradition; blue flowers on a grey glaze are typical of certain Belgian pottery.

Some packages still in use survive because the traditional excellence of the product within is identified with the vernacular package. English marmalade in its grey crock, Dijon mustard in a clay pot and many wine and liquor bottles still survive modernization. Signs painted by amateurs or sign painters with no art training are sometimes (and were in the past more frequently) examples of vernacular lettering and graphic design. Posters and handbills set by printers unaware of established design standards are similar in character although the type itself is necessarily more sophisticated in conception.

Chinese basket.

Dijon mustard crock.

Traditional Chinese dish with fish decoration.

44

Belgian crock with blue decoration on grey glaze.

Wine label of traditional vernacular character.

English marmalade pot.

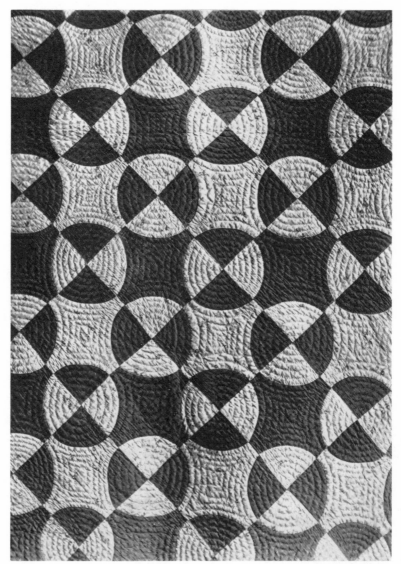

Quilt.

There are also vernacular traditions in textiles and apparel. The quilts and coverlets made by average people, without elaborate preplanning, are good examples, which sometimes exhibit an imagination and even brilliance that rivals sophisticated art. Homemade clothing, especially work clothing, may also be vernacular in character, although the influence of the fashion industry has been strong in this area for many years so that sophistication (however limited) has tended to push aside vernacular traditions.

Vernacular building was until quite recently the norm for most farm construction—barns, sheds and chicken houses. The farmhouse itself was in most cases modified by awareness of stock plans and decorative features that made it stylish. But very early and very primitive farm dwellings can be considered as examples of the vernacular. The excellence and beauty of the traditional barn is well known. It was the work of skilled carpenter-builders, often only parttime professionals, who relied on the help of owner and neighbors for such major erection steps as the raising of the main frame. Wood joints such as mortise and tenon and wood pegs are the major fastenings. Plans were not used; the members were simply cut to the desired dimensions and put up according to well-known custom. There are both regional and individual variations to suit climate, terrain, use, and particular requirements, but excellence in practical terms and in visual character is widespread. Barn red has become a traditional color, although other suitable colors (yellows, white, and bare weathered wood or shingles) are not unusual.*

Traditional wood barns, silos and sheds are now being replaced by industrially produced buildings, usually assemblies of standard elements. There is no reason why these should not be equally well designed, as demonstrated by many of the new types of silo, but in spite of the short-range economic superiorities that have made them popular, most of these new types lack the subtle excellence of the vernacular buildings.

Nautical activities have been the source of a lively vernacular for as long as there are available records to inform us. While major ships have always required some sort of skilled planning, using models and drawings and the knowledge of experts, more modest boats, rowboats, skiffs and dories, however, are true vernacular types in form, detail and, often, in color too. Fishing gear has developed much as tools have, in response to an evolutionary process of trial and error, with the best types

---

*The common vernacular color scheme for barns and farm buildings in Finland is the same red, but with doors dull black—a strikingly handsome standard.

Vernacular sign painted on a barn door.

Farm and country house design is based on vernacular traditions. Silos for grain or coal storage represent a form of vernacular architecture.

taking precedence over less successful ones and so becoming a standard norm. The lobster pots and buoys, nets, floats and coiled ropes of the small fishing harbor, along with the vernacular building of wharfs and sheds, have become favorite subjects for painters and photographers for the obvious appeal of their excellently developed forms and color.

It is not possible to set precise boundaries separating vernacular design from the design characteristics of modern technology. Over the last 120 years, industrialization has moved into every area where a vernacular was once dominant, taking command even of fields where vernacular tradition had only some minor role. The marine world, once dominated by vernacular traditions, has become increasingly technological. Railroads, one of the most characteristic of early technologies, at first incorporated their own vernacular. It was less clearly expressed in the key developments, such as locomotives and track work, than in the incidental buildings, tanks, signs, signals and accessories and in some of the details of the major equipment. Paint color schemes and lettering layouts embody the vernacular of railroading.

A cluster of rowboats.

Lobster buoys with color stripe for identification.

A railroad water tank detail.

The vernacular of railroad track. Vernacular traditions meet modern technology in such situations. Railway vernacular lettering on a freight car.

Technological objects are often full of vernacular details. Subordinate parts, wheels, plumbing and valves, instruments and tools associated with the major aspects of modern technology often retain features surviving from an earlier vernacular. There is no particular merit in trying to make sharp distinctions. What is significant to observe is that vernacular design in some ways parallels the processes of form making in nature. In so doing, it has generated innumerable successes—things that do their jobs well, are practically constructed of sensible and durable materials and, surprisingly or not, are widely accepted as beautiful and satisfying, quite aside from whatever practical values they represent.

Design in Technology

The rise of technology to a dominating role in the industrialized parts of the world, and its rapid invasion of the developing countries, is the key fact of modern history. All discussions of recent design history are dominated by the drastic changes that industrialization has brought about. It is possible to identify several successive steps in the impact of this development on the design world. A first phase might be called unconsciousness—isolation, indifference and a mild contempt for whatever might be happening in the practical world. This was the view of the stylistic revivalists and the eclectics of the nineteenth century. A second phase involved the embrace of technology, and the elevation of the machine to a godlike domination. What is usually called the modern movement in art, architecture and design is in some degree underpinned by this attitude. We are now in the midst of another phase, a reaction to worship of the machine, where the unexpected negative by-products of industrialized technology have become painfully evident. The second phase is still alive, but the new opposition characteristic of the third phase is very much in evidence.

All views which see technology either as a total solution to all problems or as an evil to be fought at all cost are, in the end, naive. Technology, as its name implies, is no more than a collection of techniques available for whatever uses it is decided to make of them. Once developed, techniques do not vanish; they remain available and confront us only with problems of what their best uses may be. It is not reasonable to assign blame to techniques for the unfortunate consequences that can arise from their ill-considered use.

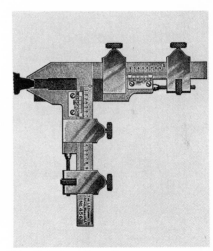

Machinists' vernier calipers.

We stand now, well along in a developmental progression that has modified and largely replaced medieval attitudes with attitudes that we characterize as modern. The medieval view was focused on the supernatural; it put no faith in what we now call rationality, and had only dim inclinations to search out relationships of cause and effect. The changes in attitude that ended the Middle Ages are still developing, but it is easy to identify the emergence of respect for the search for causal relationships. What we now call science is the resulting system for orderly search and reporting of such investigations. Science can now rest secure on the proven cases of its achievements. It has come to be taken for granted that all, or at least most, things can become known and that all (or most) things are possible if the necessary knowledge is sought out and applied.

The processes of applying scientific knowledge to practical ends is what we mean by technology. Its effectiveness has made a world totally unlike the medieval one, and, whatever its problems, a world that no one seems ready to abandon in favor of the seeming simplicity of earlier times. The purpose of this brief concentration on the products of technology is simply to search out examples of excellence in design produced by modern industrial technology. Unlike nature, and unlike vernacular design, technological design is not anonymous. There are trained and specialized experts, inventors, engineers, draftsmen and designers behind every technological achievement. We do not, for some reason, usually make stars of these people so that, although they exist and are quite readily identifiable, an illusion of anonymity hangs over this area also. When we ask who designed a tree, we know that the question is rhetorical. When we ask who designed a hammer or an axe, we know that the answer is lost in ancient and complex processes of development that cannot be related to knowable individuals. If we ask who designed a particular airplane, or bridge, or highway, there is no reason why the answer should not be available except for the modern custom that keeps these individuals out of sight, buried in most cases in the corporate bureaucracies that typically produce the modern technological object.

In some sense, almost every modern object is technological—at least in the way it is made and in the use of materials, if not in total concept. For our present purpose, however, it makes sense to concentrate on objects that might be called exclusively, or dominantly, technological. Many modern products, especially consumer products, involve mechanical, electrical or electronic internal elements, but clothe them in sur-

The Corliss engine as exhibited in Philadelphia in 1876.

faces designed to relate more clearly to art and style than to the inner technology. An automobile is technological as long as we look under the skin at wheels, frame, motor and suspension, but these elements are largely masked by the finished design of the sculptural and decorative body. The technical aspects are the work of engineers; the form is the making of stylists trained in art.

As defined here, the technological object is entirely formed by its engineering without any conscious concern for matters of external appearance or other aesthetic considerations. It would be logical to expect such objects to be ugly, or at least aesthetically neutral, while designed objects would be thought of as consistently more attractive. It is one of the strange paradoxes of modern design practice that the opposite is more often (although by no means always) the case. The goals of engineering practice—efficiency and economy—tend to promote design excellence, while the engineer's detachment from aesthetic matters insulates him from self-consciousness and the pressures of a commercial market for changing style.

It is for these reasons that technology, like nature and vernacular design, becomes a textbook or demonstration center for potential design excellence. One of the key inventions which marked the beginning of the industrial revolution was the steam engine. The early inventors and improvers used a vernacular construction related to that of simple utility buildings, carts and wagons. As invention moved into real engineering, dependent on advance planning, drawings and systematic shop methods, this vernacular blossomed into a polished and expert vocabulary. Lewis Mumford has called this vocabulary "paleo-technic," that is, early machine-age technology.* It is a vocabulary of standardized detail (such as nuts and bolts, pipes and valves) and assembled parts. An engine could be disassembled into a mass of parts and many of these parts were easily replaceable and even interchangeable between different machines. Occasionally visible parts, particularly supporting frames, were treated with architectural detail in the fashion of the time—Greek or Roman at first and then even Gothic, as fashions changed. This kind of detail was always confined to nonmoving structure. The actual working parts are invariably totally logical, taken individually, and as assembled into the working machine, make up remarkably lively patterns, particularly as seen in motion. The engine room of a factory or a ship,

Gothic details added to the engine of a side-wheel, ocean-going steamship.

*Lewis Mumford, *Technics and Civilization* (Harcourt Brace, 1934). Mumford states that this and related terms were coined by Patrick Geddes.

54

The early steam locomotive was an assembly of unrelated parts.

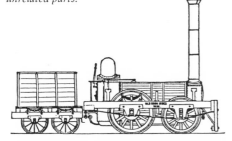

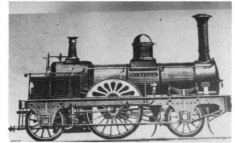

Greco-Roman details trim a railway locomotive of the 1840s.

Austere mechanical detail in the engine of a British warship, the H.M.S. Agincourt of 1868.

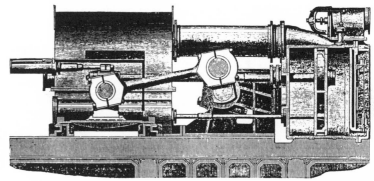

A typical locomotive from the era of dominant steam power.

Swinging drawbridge crossing the Harlem River in New York.

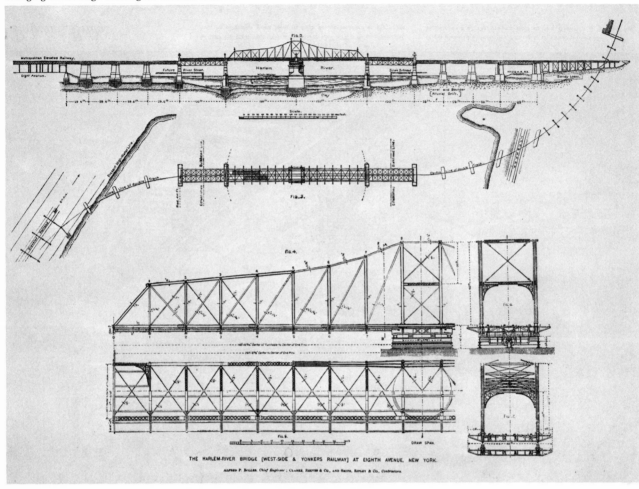

THE HARLEM-RIVER BRIDGE [WEST-SIDE & YONKERS RAILWAY] AT EIGHTH AVENUE, NEW YORK.

ALFRED P. BOLLER, *Chief Engineer*; CLARKE, REEVES & CO., AND SMITH, RIPLEY & CO., *Contractors*.

the interior of a pumping station, were often provided with windows or visitors' galleries so that the beauty and dignity of these early mechanical marvels could be easily viewed and admired.

The term engine is commonly applied to the railway locomotive, although it combines the boiler, with engine and mounts both on running wheels. The railway engine is only one part of the complex of technological designs that make up a railroad. Trackwork, signals, tanks and coaling silos, trestles and bridges all share the characteristic logic of this kind of design. Any bridge is, in some sense, technological, but the bridges of ancient Rome or the Middle Ages rely on traditional lintel or arch constructions used according to custom rather than on a basis of calculation. Nineteenth-century engineering applied scientific approaches to such construction. Tests determined the exact strengths of various materials and it became possible to calculate sizes of members to maximize efficiency. At the same time, invention of new forms for bridge structures (trusses, hinged arches, and lift-bridge types) generated a new family of bridge types. It is widely recognized that many (although by no means all) bridges are very beautiful, and one has an intuitive sense of the logic underlying these forms, making them convincing rather than arbitrary.

The Brooklyn Bridge, possibly the most admired of all suspension bridges. John and Washington Roebling, completed 1875.

Many examples of technological design are less well known and less admired; even, in some cases regarded as ugly, in spite of a comparable logic. Factories, for example, or water tanks, radio and high-tension electrical towers, would not be most people's first choice of aesthetic objects. Many such things have gained a bad reputation for secondary reasons; factories may be dirty or noisy and characterize a bad neighborhood, at least if one is thinking of residential locations. Tanks and power lines can be an intrusion in a landscape that was more natural without them. Railroads and highways can blight surrounding areas and represent a source of danger. These are not problems that are inherent in the things themselves, but have more to do with unwise locations, specific, unsolved technical problems (those associated with waste and pollution, for example) and similar side effects of the industrial revolution. Taken strictly as objects, mills and factories are often among the finest examples of the building of their times. Considered alone, tanks and towers, which go unnoticed or are regarded as ugly intrusions where they do not belong, are often superb examples of elegant and logical form. If you ignore waste, smell and effect on surroundings, chemical plants and oil refineries can be very beautiful.

At a smaller scale, the inside of a radio or television set is usually more orderly, logical and handsome than the outside; the works of a watch or clock more worthy of our attention than the case. The affection felt by hobbyists for the tools of their avocation—certain cameras, telescopes or microscopes—often turns out to be primarily a matter of admiration for the objects themselves, quite apart from their uses. Admiration approaching worship for technological things may appear absurd at times, or a matter of mistaken values, but it still in part expresses the visual power of these objects to capture human mental involvement through the strength of their forms.

We are now in a period of reaction against the excessive devotion to technology that characterized what is sometimes called the "first machine age." This was the era of first discovery and application of science to human purpose in a massive way, the period of generalized mechanization of work and transport. In our current distress about the hazards and problems that we have created, it is easy to move to reaction against the appreciation of the forms of mechanization that became so dominant in the 1920s and 1930s. The nineteenth-century American sculptor, Horatio Greenough (1805–52), who was perhaps a better theorist than sculptor, is supposed to have been the first person to suggest that "form follows function"—by which he meant that form

Town water tank at Orebro, Sweden. The tank is the tallest structure in the town and one of the best looking. The top is used for an observation platform and restaurant. Spherical water tank.

Electric transmission line tower.

Mechanism of a pocket watch of the late eighteenth century.
Nineteenth-century microscope.

The British clipper ship Cutty Sark.

Windmill in Holland.

Early Hoe ten-cylinder rotary printing press.

should follow function—and used as an example in support of his thesis the American clipper ships, outstanding examples of an early technology of his day. Le Corbusier in his famous and influential tract on architecture, *Vers une Architecture,** used early twentieth-century ships, airplanes and automobiles as examples of what architecture could and should be in his view. To accuse these men of an excessive and unreasoning worship of machinery is quite wrong and involves a misunderstanding of their messages. Both were simply pointing out things that were well designed and therefore beautiful, in periods when the nature of design excellence had become obscured in a passion for applied decoration. Neither intended to suggest that an excessive and uncontrolled application of technology had any particular merit; indeed, Le Corbusier constantly described intelligent and humane applications of technology in architecture and town planning totally different from common modern practice that has produced so many distressing results.

If this new suspicion of technology that is coming to replace the previous uncritical enthusiasm stands in the way of visual appreciation of jet aircraft, atomic power plants and super highway interchanges, it may be helpful to remember that such relatively benign objects as sewing machines, windmills, hydroelectric turbines, printing presses and medical research instruments are also technological, and no less useful, examples of design excellence.

One further matter needs clarification in any discussion of the character of technological design. This has to do with the role of imagination and what is now usually called creativity in the design of technological objects. It is often asserted that such things *must* be well designed because their design is dictated by pressures of realities beyond human control. It is, of course, true that all design is subject to some such pressure. There is no escape from the law of gravity and the laws of physics. The notion that such pressures lead to one inevitable result as the only solution to each problem cannot be sustained. Aircraft are often cited in such discussion. An airplane can only be of a certain shape, it is often said, because it must be of a shape that will make it possible for it to fly. In this view, the aeronautical engineer is seen as helpless, forced by his slide rule and computer to generate an inevitable form, quite beyond human control. By contrast, everyday objects, such as chairs, with less demanding performance requirements, can take on almost any form a

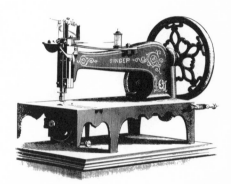

Early sewing machine.

*(Paris, 1923). Titled *Toward a New Architecture* in its English translation.

Robert Maillart bridge across the river Thur.

Stirling "single" locomotive.

designer may wish to give them. A comparison of this sort includes some valid points—failure in a chair is less total and less dramatic. One can sit on a rocker or on a Louis XVI sofa with almost equal comfort, but one cannot fly about on a rock (or on a sofa, for that matter). The performance we expect of many simple things is relatively unspecific and not very demanding, while it is in the nature of the technological product that it must perform to very exacting specifications, often quite hard to meet. There is no question that this changes the role of the designer from that of a rather free and relaxed maker of shapes to that of a very narrowly constrained user of complex information. This does not however, in any way, put into the hands of the technological designer the solutions that he seeks. The form of every airplane must be invented just as much as the form of every chair; the difference is only that the tests of success are much more rigorous. Any doubt about this should be dispelled by the astonishing variety in technological designs for a given purpose. Aircraft differ in design as much as chairs. A certain type may become standard for a specific function in a specific time context because its proven success discourages experiment in other directions. But sooner or later a new form will surface, newly invented as a better solution to an old problem.

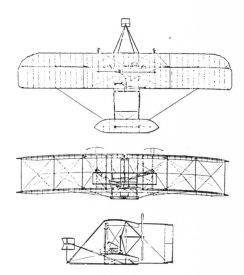

Wright Brothers "Flyer."

The process of engineering design is really no different from any other design process; it involves the proposal of a solution to a problem, generated out of knowledge of past efforts, applicable scientific principles and some further element of imagination that we call creativity. The proposal is then subject to evaluation through simple critical observation, through calculation, through tests of parts, models and similar partial realizations, and finally, tests of an actual sample or prototype. The evaluative testing may lead to improvement of the original concept or to its rejection, and may suggest directions for a new proposal, but the proposal itself is still always an individual human achievement. This explains why personal style can emerge even in the most demanding of engineering work. The tradition of anonymity in such fields somewhat conceals this fact, but where this tradition has been broken, engineering design can be seen to be almost as personal as art. The locomotives of Patrick Stirling, the airplanes of the Wright Brothers and the bridges of Robert Maillart are each so special to their designers that visual identification of a previously unknown example would be easy for anyone who knew even one typical example. It may also explain why it is that some technological designs command such an intense degree of interest, loyalty and enthusiasm, even when they do not equal the designs of nature, or surpass those of certain vernacular traditions.

Examination of the admirable situations we find in nature, in examples of vernacular and technological design is only useful if it is possible to extract some generalizations that can be applied outside these areas. Efforts to extract such generalizations have been in progress for a long time and we know about them, in most cases, because of the efforts of architects to develop a theoretical framework for their activities. Until recently, buildings were the largest, most costly and most important of human artifacts, and the people who designed them approached their work with considerable professionalism, even as long ago as 4,000 years. The difference between better and worse buildings has surely been apparent as long as any building activity has been known. The urge to explain, clarify and discuss this difference must also have surfaced very long ago. But we are dependent on written documentation for our knowledge of past theories of excellence in architecture, and such data from the earliest eras of major building have not been preserved.

The writer on architectural practice whose works have come down to us from the earliest time is Vitruvius, a Roman architect-engineer who in the first century B.C. put together in his *Ten Books on Architecture* everything that a good Roman architect might want to know. Vitruvius was more a practical man than a theorist and devoted most of his books to solid practical advice about brick, stone and mixing lime, and rules for producing temples, houses and sundials in the most accepted fashion of the day. His efforts to codify the bases for excellence in architecture are limited to a few sentences in his introduction to his first book. In chapter 2, he tells us that "architecture depends on Order, Arrangement, Eurythmy, Symmetry, Propriety and Economy."* In chapter 3, these rather esoteric concepts are summarized in the phrase, "All these must be built with due reference to durability, convenience and beauty." In the absence of any other texts dealing in any way with architecture, Vitruvius's books exerted a remarkable degree of influence, particularly in the Renaissance, when interest in anything surviving from ancient Rome became intense. Various versions of Vitruvius became current in print shortly after the printing press was developed and translations into various languages were attempted.

Sir Henry Wotton (1568–1639) published in 1624 *The Elements of Architecture,* which is derived fairly directly from Vitruvius. Wotton was not an architect but a lawyer—what we would now call a diplomat—and a poet. It may have been this last skill that led him to convert Vitruvius's words about "convenience, durability and beauty" into the quaint and memorable sentence, "Well-building hath three qualities, commodity, firmness and delight." This phrase has entered into the literature of architecture in a way that has turned it into a cliché, in danger of becoming laughable through excessive repetition.

Overquoted or not, the thought that Vitruvius and/or Wotton organized so neatly, remains a useful and fundamental basis for all theoretical discussion of architecture and the other aspects of design that have taken on comparable importance in modern times. The quaint phrases of Wotton can be translated as "good design (or good architecture) has three aspects: functional utility, structure and aesthetics," which, if not as pleasant a sentence to read, brings the same ideas into a modern context.

Function, a favorite word among design critics and a key slogan of the modern movement means, of course, filling an intended purpose. Utilitarian things are made to *do* something specific, perform in some intended way, and their success in these terms depends on how they are designed. Structure is not quite as clear a concept. We do not have one clear word (like "firmness") to summarize wise selection of materials, logical assembly into sturdy and durable objects, respect for problems of craftsmanship and manufacturing technology, including questions of reasonable economy, and all the other issues that together qualify for the label "well made" or "well built." Even without a single word, it is clear that this is a group of related issues that are vital to any design success. The last aspect of the three qualities—delight or, in modern

*As given in the translation of the *Ten Books on Architecture,* by Morris Hicky Morgan (Harvard University Press, 1914).

66

terms, aesthetics—is the most troublesome and leads into some complex and tangled philosophical questions. It is nevertheless clear that this is an aspect of design that is universally recognized as significant and that is not quite the same as (although certainly related to) matters of function and structure.

If we ask what else design involves, we find that the various criteria that come to mind can usually be subsumed by one of the historic three. Economy, for example, can be an aspect of functional requirements and is achieved through appropriate choice of materials and construction techniques. Safety is certainly an aspect of function as is environmental impact. If we try to reduce this three-part analysis to a smaller number of aspects, we find ourselves involved in semantic juggling, in which we might define aesthetic function, for example, in so limited a way that it becomes possible to sweep the aesthetic issues into the functional department. Verbal rearrangement of concepts of this kind does not really alter the usefulness of the old conceptual structure.

It seems then useful here to look more carefully at these three aspects of design as they relate not only to architecture, but to every other kind of design undertaken by human beings in the contemporary world. If the three topics overlap and interlace, that only reassures us that together they describe the organic wholes that all humanly designed things must necessarily be. The first of the three, Vitruvius's "convenience," Wotton's "commodity" and the modern "function," seem the most clear and obvious, but includes some subtle complexities that may not be evident on first examination.

Functional Design

The concept of *function* has become very central to all thought about design in the contemporary world. *Functionalism,* a doctrine better known through the attacks leveled against it than through any clear statements of its adherents, is commonly represented as the view which maintains that the forms of objects can, should, or must be determined strictly by the requirements of their functional performance. The slogan, "form follows function," discussed earlier as a phrase coined by Horatio Greenough, but most often attributed to Louis Sullivan—who was actually merely quoting Greenough—is said to be the central idea behind functionalism. In spite of having quoted the phrase, Sullivan is not in any way an example of the typical functionalist. He was an imaginative and individualistic architect whose personal style of decoration was an important part of his work. The functionalist is, according to the usual understanding of the term, expected to avoid personal expression and, above all, any elements as willful and nonfunctional as decoration.

The word function itself has a curious character: it seems more heavy, more technical and more oppressive than such possible alternatives as use, usefulness, utility or purpose. It has, nonetheless, become the favorite professional term for defining the aspects of an object's intentions that might be called specifically purposeful. Works of fine art—painting, sculpture, music or poetry—are not regarded as functional in this narrow sense because their purposes cannot be defined in terms of immediate utility. We do not expect these things to perform services for us of a practical and immediately definable sort. In contrast, useful objects are expected to provide services of a clearly identifiable physical sort, such as shelter, transport, convenience, mechanical advantage or some similar kind of easily recognizable utility. What we expect a thing to do is, in this sense, its function.

To say, then, that we expect useful objects to function and to function well becomes something of a platitude. A bottle opener must open bottles, a screw driver, drive screws, a ship, sail and an airplane, fly in order to justify their existence, and it becomes difficult to visualize a modern designer so dense as to neglect these points. Failure at so basic a level of requirement as this, does, of course, occur occasionally, but it is generally understood that this is a result of some error or mistake in development, not in original intention. The most basic idea of functionalism—the view that a thing must do what it is intended to do—can be seen to be almost universally accepted. That a universally accepted view should become the heart of a powerful new theory—moreover, one that is hotly contested—seems in some way absurd, and yet that is what has happened in the theoretical literature of architecture and design over the last fifty years.

The background of this absurdity lies in historical developments of the nineteenth century, the beginning of the industrial revolution. No other comparably short period of human history has ever been so dedicated to the creation of functional objects, things that would perform one service or another with efficiency and to the advantage of its human inventors and users. This dedication has created for us the vast repertoire of functionally effective products that we call technological and discussed earlier as one of the key sources for design direction in modern times. In the nineteenth and early twentieth centuries and even

68

now, to some extent, these technological objects have been regarded with some degree of hostility by their human users. Much as they are embraced for their performance capacity, they embody qualities that seem less than acceptable emotionally. This was probably particularly true at the beginnings of the industrial revolution when machinery, materials like iron and steel, chemical processes and all the associated problems of industrialism were seen as totally strange and threatening whatever might be their demonstrable technical advantages. We know that power looms, horseless carriages and steamboats were all resisted and more or less directly attacked as dangerous, harmful and objectionable alterations in an accepted, traditional way of life.

The nineteenth century was a period of overwhelming ambiguity. Public attitudes of stiff morality lived alongside secret vice. Religion was dominant as announced doctrine, but behavior was full of cruelties and selfish aggressions that, in concept, are hardly equalled even in modern times. It is not surprising, then, that the Victorian view of design was inclined to accept the advantages of the technology of the industrial revolution, but attempted to conceal such realities under a veil somewhat like the public religiosity and morality that was used to screen the hard realities of colonialism, wars of imperialism and the general exploitation of agricultural and industrial lower classes. The essence of nineteenth-century design was the concealment of reality. Machinery was meant to be out of sight, in the basement or out at the back. Structure was a hidden reality to be clothed in ornament that would make its hard facts unnoticeable. The human body was, insofar as possible, denied any existence hidden in the elaboration of modest clothing. Work was to be done out of sight, in mills, mines and "black towns" that could be ignored by tasteful and educated people, who could concentrate instead on the affectations of Victorian art and decoration.

This background puts functionalism into a more logical context as a revolutionary doctrine, a return to the obvious which had become so nonobvious as to require an almost violent round of changes to make it visible again. Buildings and machinery clothed in Greek and Gothic trim had become so commonplace as to seem normal. Everything was, said to represent a style; every building, every piece of furniture, every utilitarian article was made an opportunity for applied art, laid on quite literally as a surface frosting entirely unrelated to realities of utility.

In this context, it was quite natural that reformist architects and designers would need to restate the obvious and, possibly, even to overstate it. Le Corbusier when he stated that "a house is a machine for

Decorative detail of Louis Sullivan's Bayard Building in New York.

living" probably intended to be shocking, but he was also trying to reassert a rationality that seemed to have been lost in the excesses of late nineteenth- and early twentieth-century decoration. A house had always, until then, been a device, a shelter, an apparatus for living. The vocabulary of the machine as the method by which the best and most effective devices were created, applied to a house should not, therefore, have seemed revolutionary. That it did so is only a reflection of the obscurity into which such logical views had fallen. In order to illustrate his points, Le Corbusier had to turn to ships, airplanes, bridges and grain elevators as examples. The buildings to illustrate his points were either from earlier history (most often ancient Greek) or were his own newly designed works.

None of the pioneer modernists of the 1920s actually asserted a doctrine of *pure* functionalism. This is a concept that has a rather cloudy history—in fact, it is not clear that it has ever been voiced by anyone except its detractors who have been vocal in setting it up in order to knock it down again. In this purported view, function—that is to say, utility—is supposed to dictate every aspect of the design of a thing. Mechanical objects are supposed to exemplify this kind of design process, and it is claimed that the pure functionalist intends to proceed to the design of more commonplace objects, most often buildings, in the same way. The modern architecture of the 1920s and 1930s with its flat roofs, large glass areas, smooth white wall surfaces and slim columns of modern materials (steel and concrete) is supposed to be purely functional. Family resemblances to industrial plants, aircraft hangers among buildings, to machines and scientific apparatus among smaller objects is regarded as symptomatic of this functionalist direction. Such work is customarily attacked by its detractors on two, rather curiously contradictory grounds: (1) that it is not truly as functional as it pretends (flat roofs leak, white walls crack and look shabby, glass walls limit privacy, and so on) and (2) that in being functional, other values— emotional, aesthetic and generally humane—are neglected and suppressed. As we gain the perspective of time in our view of the early works of modern designers, it becomes more and more clear to almost every viewer that these works are not and were not intended to be *purely* functional. Sullivan and Wright used decoration freely, developed highly personal styles of expression and (particularly in Wright's case) were exponents of an organic (as opposed to mechanistic) way of designing. Le Corbusier and Mies van der Rohe were exponents of aesthetic systems: in the case of Le Corbusier, very explicitly

70

The Bauhaus at Dessau, by Walter Gropius, 1925.

Le Corbusier's drawing of the interior of an artist's studio-residence.

developed in his "Modulor"*; in Mies's case, obvious in the austere simplification of form characteristic of his work. In none of these men's works (nor in the works of any of the other major leaders of the movement) is it possible to identify a functionalist approach that rules out all that is personal, intuitive and nonrational.

What distinguishes modern design and architecture from what went before is acceptance of the idea that nonfunctional (or perhaps we should say antifunctional) design is objectionable. The elimination of applied decoration, the pointless overlay of floral carving on utilitarian objects and of building details derived from historic architecture frees the designer from his preoccupation with this kind of extraneous art, enabling him to look again at functional realities that are the starting point for his work. It is easy to assume that this particular battle for logic has been won—we do not build so many libraries and post offices wrapped in Roman columns and approachable only up mountains of steps as we used to. We have by no means given up comparable absurdities, however.

*Modulor I and Modulor II (Harvard University Press).

72

Imitation wood-grain panels on the sides of automobiles, colonial maple living room furniture, fixed shutters that could not cover the mobile home windows they border even if they were hinged, television sets disguised as Renaissance credenzas, are all evidences of the durability of the Victorian preference for the surface application of a gloss of prettiness rather than concern for the more difficult realities that lie beneath.

If we go beyond the historical issues that surround the concept of functionalism and ask what the realities of function have to do with the design of things, we find some rather obvious truths and a few more subtle complications. It is a truism to say that useful objects are invented, designed and made to be of use. A starting point for their design must then be consideration of what this use is. The names of objects are often definitions of intended use: a sewing machine, an egg beater, a lawn mower. There is no need for research to discover what such things are intended to do. Even such simple examples turn out to be a bit more complex than might at first appear. Is the sewing machine for industrial or home use? Is it to be portable? Will electric power be available where it is to be used? A myriad of such questions needs to be asked and answered if the resulting object is to be truly serviceable in its intended

Mies van der Rohe's drawing of the interior of a projected museum for Berlin.

use. In the mass distribution patterns of modern industrialized society, the user of an object does not normally have direct contact with the maker, and the maker can remain indifferent to the individual users' needs as long as his product will satisfy *some* users. To produce a sewing machine for home or factory use, portable or not, for electric or manual power are all reasonable plans as long as there is need for each of these differing types. The architect commissioned by an individual client to design a particular building, the craftsman asked to make a single object, can explore functional requirements in a very specific way since he can ask his client or customer what is needed. When the architect must design for a more general user public (as when designing a hotel, a school or an apartment house), or when the craftsman opens a shop selling, let us say, tables and chairs to anyone who may come in, the nature of functional requirements shifts to something less specific and therefore less helpful as a guide, but also less constraining. The craftsman can make kitchen chairs and tables, folding chairs and tables or any other types he may choose and can still expect to find a market. Site permitting, the architect can design high buildings or low, windowed or windowless, in an infinite variety of plans and materials and still satisfy quite well some part of the total user population. Any attempt to *totally* satisfy all potential users will become, in either case, quite impossible.

In all such cases the designer must, with the help of whatever information he can obtain and his own imagination, make some assumptions about what users his work will serve, and proceed on the basis of these assumptions. When we remember that things are designed at a certain time and in a particular place, but that they last for years and are, in many cases, transportable anywhere, it becomes clear that developing designs to suit *exact* requirements of function is usually out of the question.

Many of the most useful of things are useful because of their versatility.

A knife will cut anything, a hammer will pound whatever the user chooses to pound, a house will shelter any individual or group that goes inside it. A building built as a warehouse may be converted to become an apartment house. Highly specialized purposes, on the other hand, impose more exacting requirements. Only a moving-picture camera will make moving pictures; a cross-cut saw is not ideal for cutting with the grain; an atomic power plant will not easily convert for use as a hotel. Functional requirements can range up and down such scales of generalization versus precision and many cases of dissatisfaction with objects stem from a mismatch between need and product in these terms. A versatile knife (a folding pocketknife, for example) will serve almost any purpose for which a knife is useful with some success, but may not be ideal for such highly specialized uses as surgical operations or cutting mortises for hinges. A scalpel or a carpenter's chisel, each excellent for its own purpose, are not so handy if one must carry only one knife on a camping trip.

Although one normally thinks of intended use as a preexisting and determining factor, leading to the object created, it is possible to observe reverse cases. Inventors of the violin, for example, could hardly have had in mind the literature that was eventually written to be played on that instrument. They were, rather, free experimenters with the making of sounds, and as the instruments came to be known, their usefulness was developed by the composers and players who gradually expanded or created the full function of the existing instrument. Since invention is inherently a more generalized process, it follows this pattern more often than design. The inventors of the airplane must have had some general notion about its future potential, but their work was primarily concentrated on getting it off the ground. Today, the designer of a particular airplane will need to know what it is to carry, how far and how fast, what landing places it will use and dozens of other detailed requirements in order to design a specific manifestation of the airplane species.

Simplistic discussions of function in design often lose sight of the complexity of multiple functional requirements that characterize the development of most modern objects. If one supposes that each thing has *a* function, it can seem that discussions of this matter are pointless. The definition of a chair, after all, requires that any chair can be sat in. Similarly, all knives must cut, airplanes fly, and failure in this kind of primary function dooms an object to total failure and, in all probability, to the junk heap. In practice, every object has, in addition to the obvious primary function, many other subsidiary functional characteristics. Not only must it be sittable, cut or fly as the case may be, but it must also be comfortable to use, safe, the right weight, easy to maintain and not too expensive in first cost and maintenance. An object of any complexity can generate long lists of such secondary requirements which will be of varied importance and may, in many cases, be in conflict. "Strong enough" is often in conflict with "light enough" and both can be in conflict with "not too costly."

In modern practice, the searching out and inventory of *all* requirements and the development of some view of their relative importance (as essential, desirable or incidental, for example) has come to be known as programming, an activity that can take place before design is attempted and that can be immeasurably helpful in the design process. People often go so far as to say that once a really complete program has been prepared, design becomes almost automatic—an overstatement obviously since no two designers would be likely to propose identical, or even closely similar, solutions to the problem set forth in a particular program. Assuming that each designer produced a design that satisfied the given program, the differences in proposals must be the result of differences in each one's assessment of priorities and to the influence of individual experience and preferences. The more precise and constraining the requirements of program and the more demanding the environmental and physical constraints within which an object must perform, the less leeway there is for significant differences in individual design approaches. It is striking that most jet transport aircraft are similar, those of a given size and range so alike as to often be difficult to distinguish. This is the result of such demanding constraints.* In contrast, the design of single family houses is infinitely varied—they may involve even more functional requirements, but there is a wider range of ways in which they can be satisfied.

Within recent years there has been some effort to make the steps from functional requirement to design proposal more systematic and orderly and, it is hoped, more effective than has been the case in the past. Christopher Alexander in various papers and in a book, *Notes on the Synthesis of Form* (Harvard University Press, 1964), has outlined a system for listing all discoverable functional requirements for a given need (he lists twenty-one for a tea kettle in an example), and then studying interactions between requirements in an effort to group them in related clusters that can be studied together. These clusters can then be brought into a hierarchical order of relationships until the final design proposal emerges. Many designers still doubt the usefulness of so elaborate a theoretical approach, but many modern projects are so complex that anything less systematic will almost inevitably mean that some considerations are neglected or that some conflicts are not adequately resolved. Alexander uses as a "worked example" the design of an entire

* In this case there is an additional factor discouraging varied approaches: the great cost in time and money involved in developing any new direction. Aeronautical engineers prefer to build on past successes rather than to strike out in new directions.

new village to be constructed in India. The long lists of complex interactive requirements make it clear how difficult the management of such design projects can be in terms of functional needs alone.

A problem that surfaces when Alexander's (and other similar) methodological approaches are applied, has to do with the difficulty in assigning values for relative importance to different functional requirements. A simple example will make this issue clear. In planning a house, it is desirable to have windows face toward the best view. It is also desirable that windows should face away from the road or street for quiet and privacy. On a lot where the best view is across the road, a conflict results between the two requirements. If the designer is working for an individual client, he can ask for an expression of preference and act accordingly, although many clients might have difficulty in arriving at a decision about such an issue. A decision to favor the view and deal with the privacy issue by whatever palliatives may be discoverable could generate an acceptable design, as could the decision to ignore the view and face the house on an internal garden. Assigning equal values to two such conflicting needs could, on the other hand, produce a house that had both limited view and poor privacy. Anyone who has tried to use rating scales to evaluate people, automobiles or anything else has discovered that the best score is often made by the candidate that is indifferent in every way. In practice, one outstanding strength can compensate for a number of weaknesses in other areas. Most designers seem to have an intuitive understanding of this and will choose the functional requirements that they wish to favor in some kind of priority order. This probably explains the well-known fact that many drastically different designs can be good solutions to the same problem. One can choose any one of a number of chairs, lamps, automobiles or lawn mowers, each different in appearance and in some functional characteristics, but all virtually equal in overall merit.

Christopher Alexander's "tree diagram" from Notes on the Synthesis of Form

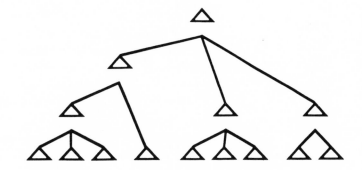

This kind of variation which results from designers and users placing differing values on various functional requirements generates some random variation among even the best designs of a given type. A comparison with comparable situations in nature is, of course, suggested. Each animal (including the human animal) appears in a range of differing size, shape and color, even though all of a given species are biologically identical. In biology, this random variation is considered an aspect of the process of natural selection in which alternatives to a basic standard are, in effect, tested for survival advantage over the extremely long spans of biological time. In the making of human artifacts, there is a comparable process—much more rapid, and more superficial in its effectiveness. Different variants of a certain object type will gradually yield to the evolution of the most generally satisfactory variant which emerges as a standard, until some new need or new discovery alters the context and generates a new cycle of development.

It is not surprising, then, that excellence in functional terms is not an absolute quality. One user may be best satisfied with an object that favors function A, another user with a similar object that favors function B. An automobile should be easy to drive and comfortable to ride in. The first requirement suggests small size, hard springs and quick steering and braking; the second suggests a big body, soft springs and more gentle response to controls. A design based on either set of priorities can be satisfactory to a large number of people, and debates about which is best become somewhat pointless—we must ask "best for what?" We can still be certain that an automobile so hard to drive that it is dangerous, or so uncomfortable that a few minutes ride will be exhausting will be unsatisfactory—not functional at even a minimum level and so not, in those terms, a satisfactory design.

Before attempting some general conclusions about these issues, it is necessary to examine two more situations that can lead to some confused and fruitless discussion. If an object, designed in a way that one has every reason to expect to be practical and workable, is then *made* in a way that introduces troublesome, even disastrous, problems, it is not logical to insist that its failure to function satisfactorily is evidence of bad design. An automobile of excellent design can be equipped with an engine that will break down in a short time for internal, technical reasons. One might argue that the mechanical design of the engine is defective (although it could also be a matter of manufacturing errors or faulty materials), but the overall design of the vehicle would not be at issue. In contrast, an automobile designed in a way that distributes weights so unevenly as to make safe handling impossible, or that obstructs the driver's vision, suffers from genuine functional *design* deficiencies that cannot be corrected without some alteration of the vehicle's basic form. It is not uncommon to find in modern products (up to and including buildings and even towns) otherwise excellently designed, some technical deficiency that renders the object useless as a whole. An office building with windows that snap out in a high wind is not, for that reason, necessarily badly designed in any basic way—it may merely need a better window frame detail—but until this matter is dealt with, the entire building can be considered useless.

One more obvious point needs to be restated. Satisfactory, even excellent functional performance is not, in itself, any guarantee of overall design excellence. One can sit comfortably in an unsightly chair, tell time by a clock made to resemble a teapot, enjoy music emanating from a radio concealed in a pseudo-Renaissance chest. Conversely, chair, clock or radio will not be satisfactory useful objects, however attractive their appearance, if their design makes them impossible to sit in, difficult to tell time by or impossible to tune. To put the matter differently, functional failure resulting from ill-conceived design is indicative of general design failure. Functional success stands as a first step, but only a first step, toward general design success.

The generalizations that can be extracted from this line of reasoning might be summarized as follows:

1. Any utilitarian object must be designed so that it will serve its intended purpose, at least at some minimal level that can be considered satisfactory.

2. Satisfactory performance is never an absolute quality. It can only be evaluated in relative terms. A *more* satisfactory solution to a problem is always possible and is, by definition, better.

3. Satisfactory performance is invariably a matter of meeting a number of requirements—a vast number in the case of complex designs. The various requirements may be in conflict so that different satisfactory solutions can result from differing emphases on differing requirements. One *most* satisfactory solution only can emerge in the limited context of one particular evaluation of the relative importance of various desiderata.

4. Failure in relation to the points listed above leads to overall failure of any design; a degree of success is a condition of general design success, but does not assure it. Other issues, interactive with function, are also of vital importance.

Structures, Materials and Techniques

It would seem logical to begin discussion of the design of *useful* objects with considerations of utility, but one cannot effectively study this subject, except by looking at real, physical objects, put together from real materials. An abstract principle such as rigidity through triangulation, mechanical advantage gained through a lever, or conversion of electrical energy into light can be the basic key to solution to a problem. In practice, the principle can do nothing by itself. It must be used as the basis for a *design* and this involves proposing ways in which known substances can be shaped and assembled into a *thing* which will convert the underlying principle (or principles) into realizable action.

We do not have one word that summarizes this aspect of design as neatly as function expresses purpose, since different words are used for different ways of making things. One can speak of construction, of manufacturing or simply of making, implying by these terms building through assembly of parts (as in architecture), factory processes, or hand-craft techniques. Selection of materials is involved in each case but the words lead us to think of material and construction as separate, however closely related, matters. Construction and the related terms suggest the process or the techniques through which materials are converted to a finished object, while structure is a useful word to describe the conceptual nature of an object's physical reality apart from the processes used to make it. One might say of a simple building that the material is wood, the construction is on-site carpentry and that the structure is a braced frame. In common usage, such distinctions are often blurred in a way that in a sense recognizes the inseparable nature of these matters. In contrast, function is easy to separate. When we say that the simple building is a garage, we are talking only of its use and no clue is given to how it is built.

It is this ease of conceptual separation that has led to the habit of making "materials and methods" study distinct from "problem solving" in the functional sense, however illogical this separation may be. An abstract, formal solution can easily become a nonsolution if conversion into physical reality is impossible or unsuccessful. The vernacular designer and the craftsman who is also his own designer automatically work with these two aspects of design in close interrelationship. More complex technology sometimes tends to bring about separations that can be hurtful to design success. As the modern technology of steel and reinforced concrete construction first came to be applied to building, architects tended to leave these matters to engineers and to concern themselves only with planning and what was regarded as aesthetic form. As a result we can now examine (and still quite often produce) buildings in which the actual materials seem to have no role in the conceptual design. The engineer must struggle to find ways to hold the building up, then to hide what he has done, while the architect concerns himself with materials only to the extent of selecting a surface of stone (for a Gothic skyscraper) or of red brick (for a Georgian bank or courthouse). The eclectic architecture of the early twentieth century is the most dramatic example of this curiously schizophrenic split in design, but comparable absurdities are not uncommon in many other kinds of design. Contemporary products are full of simulated leather, printed imitation wood grain and metallic-finish plastics. The issue here is not a matter of whether these finishes are or are not suitable, but simply that the *actual* materials and ways of working them are considered as unimportant and incidental to the formation of the design.

Historically, there are not many instances of broad neglect or suppression of constructive techniques and the materials they use. An ancient clay pot, a Greek vase and an American Indian pottery object all share an understanding that the object's design derives in part from its intended use, but in equally large part from its material and the way that material is worked. The surface glaze, the color and patterns added to the surface (whether abstract or in some degree illustrative and naturalistic) are never allowed to overwhelm, conceal or run counter to the basic material and technique of manufacture. The pyramids derive their forms in part from the stone from which they are built and the builders' ways of using that stone. A Japanese house is as much a study in the use of wood (and secondary materials such as straw and paper) as it is a device for sheltering a certain pattern of life. Good tools and implements result from the use of metal, wood and newer materials in ways that take advantage of their characteristics. The head of a wooden mallet is different from a metal hammer head because the materials are different, as much as because their intended uses are different. One could reproduce a wooden mallet in steel, or a carpenter's hammer in wood, but the resulting tools would be useless absurdities. The pyramids reconstructed in wood and stucco, a Japanese house built of aluminum and plastic become illogical and only imaginable as exhibits in a side show.

It is important to notice that the issue here is not one of *exposed* materials. Much pointless discussion about the "honest" use of materials centers on an idea that materials, and even structural systems, should show at the external surface of an object—that finishes covering what is beneath are in some way undesirable. Some of the negative cases cited above and others that come to mind quite readily may, for a moment, seem to support this idea. It *is* absurd to wrap a steel and concrete building in a thin veneer of stone, to top a steel automobile body with simulated (plastic) leather, to trim a plastic and metal camera with wood-grained trim. To leap from this reasonable conclusion to an insistence that the steel frame of a building must always be visible on its exterior, that a steel automobile body should never be painted but left to rust naturally, or that cameras should have their mechanism exposed to view and dust externally is not reasonable at all. Covering and enclosure are useful elements of a wide variety of objects. Protection from dirt and weather are very real requirements. The normal colors and textures of some materials may not be ideal as they show up in use. Choice of surface materials and finishes is as much a part of the designers' constructive obligation as is choice of basic structural techniques. Those choices should, however, derive from the realities of practical necessity and from the characteristics of the structural and physical realities that serve those needs. If left exposed, each material will show a characteristic color and develop a characteristic finish which may be fairly stable (weathered wood) or an aspect of progressive damage (rusting iron or steel). In the first case, finishes are a means of modifying the inevitable visual characteristics of the material, in the second case a necessary protective step which forces a choice of surface appearance characteristics. If we must paint bare steel to preserve it from rust, we must also choose our color. There is no real reason to regard red lead paint, rust-color paint, aluminum paint or any other choice as inherently natural to steel.

In many cases, there are also a number of practical reasons why structural elements should be in concealed locations. Nature offers such striking examples as the skeletons of animals. There are, of course, animals with external structure, but many others (including the human animal) have skeletons which the evolutionary process has found it best to locate internally. Muscle, fat, skin and fur form layers over internal skeletal structure, but do not truly disguise it in the sense of denying its existence. The forms of animals, particularly in motion, are based on, and highly revealing of, the skeletal structure beneath. Manmade things often have such internal structure with similar reasons for covering layers, but they do not always succeed in finding the same logic of relationship. Covering layers often need an external surface skin or protective layer with functions of its own that require a special color or pattern. A comparison with natural growth is relevant here. Skins or surface membranes are a special layer, not simply a place where inner material meets outer air, and they may be uniquely colorful or patterned. In nature this is an integral part of the development of the organism, not an afterthought or cover-up intended to conceal or distort. Even the rather special example of natural camouflage exists for the real survival advantage of the species. Skin color and pattern can have the same or related roles in manmade objects, but often appear instead with less justifiable purposes: to make poorly made things appear better than they are, to disguise one material, to suggest another in order to confuse and misinform the naive observer. Chrome plating may be an ideal protective skin for metal that would otherwise rust or corrode; a simulated chrome plate on a plastic object is usually used with an intent to mislead, to suggest that the material is something different from what it really is.

Sound relationships between the design process and the structure and materials of designed objects demand that the invention or selection of structure and the selection of structural and surface materials be an integral part of the process of design. The idea that it is possible to invent a form first and then select structure and material as a later step, leads to divisions between these closely related aspects of design that almost surely defeat success. But this divisive way of doing things is actually quite commonplace. A house can be planned first and a decision to build in wood or in brick made later. A chair that has for years been made of wood can be duplicated in plastic. Developed in this way, the house design can never really exploit the qualities of its material and constructional system; the "translated" chair will be a curiosity, rather than a coherent design, even if it is, in a practical sense, serviceable. In many cases, new materials can, of course, replace older ones to advantage, but if the substitution is made without any other design adjustment, the results are invariably a disappointment.

The designer's relationship with the techniques by which things are made is, if anything, even more complex. Traditionally, full knowledge of the crafts and skills involved in making a thing was expected of a designer. The potter who designed ceramics did so while actually making them with his own hands. An architect was a master builder who had learned his profession on construction sites. Modern technology has made this kind of direct knowledge less universally available. The variety and complexity of available techniques has made it impossible for each designer to have complete and detailed knowledge of every possibility, while the rate of developmental change makes such knowledge obsolete in such short order, as to discourage the effort to be fully informed about a wide range of production methods. Nonetheless, design undertaken without concern for techniques is generally unworkable and likely to produce unsatisfactory results.

The large general issue involved in production techniques concerns the connected (but not identical) questions of whether a thing is to be made by hand or by machine, singly, in very small or very large quantity through mass production. There is some unclarity in the understanding and use of these phrases. Handmade things are usually made with the help of tools and equipment—hammers, saws, looms and potters wheels, many of which can now be mechanized to some degree. The use of a motor-driven potter's wheel or a power saw can still be part of hand work. Used in this connection, the term "machine" usually refers to a mechanical device that, once started, does its work with only minimal supervision. A power loom must be set up by hand, but once turned on will weave yardage until it runs out of material or breaks down. Similarly, in the distinction between individual and mass production, quantity is not the key issue from the design point of view. A large quantity of things can be made one by one but will not exemplify mass production, but more accurately, serial production, which isolates each step of production at the station of a particular worker or machine, so that objects pass from station to station on an assembly or production line. This latter way of making things is known to everyone as the secret of Henry Ford's efficient production of automobiles, and as the basic concept of most modern industry. Machinery and serial production have a natural affinity and most often appear together, but it is *possible* although unusual for objects to be hand made in quantity on an assembly line, or to be machine made in quantities as small as one.

All of this becomes important in design because the anticipated techniques of production set limits on what is easy and what is possible. Hand work can sometimes accomplish things too difficult for existing machines, while machines can deliver precision and replication difficult to maintain with the hand. When quantity production is desired, machines can usually perform almost any operation more economically than is possible with hand work. Once industrialized quantity production is anticipated, design must be adjusted to this reality. A metal part to be cast in an automatic die-casting machine or a plastic object to be injection molded, must be designed to take account of the realities of these processes. When a mold opens, the molded object must have been shaped so that it will release from the mold. Whether this shape is functionally ideal or regarded as aesthetic may be important, but unless the demands of the production technique have been considered, production simply cannot take place.

In the 1920s and 1930s, the first generation of modern designers were much aware of these issues and, in most cases, designed in ways that they felt made best use of modern industrial materials and production techniques. Ironically, their work was often hand produced in small quantity (often in the minimal quantity of one unit), while actual quantity production was devoted to making simulations of handmade objects. The buildings of Le Corbusier or Walter Gropius were designed with the characteristics of industrial production in mind, but were built by hand, often with considerable difficulty. The mass-produced textiles, dishes and furniture that factories were pouring out during the very same years simulated craft production and decoration.

It is easy to regard these phenomena of the 1920s and 1930s as curious, but we have not escaped from such problems. We still produce many artifacts that are conceived as expressive of industrialized technology by means of archaic hand crafts (major buildings are the most striking examples) while the products of genuine industrialization (mobile homes, for example) are distorted to make reference to preindustrial techniques. Factories make random width, knotty pine panels, small pane colonial windows and shutters and handcarved furniture on assembly lines, while gleaming glass and metal skyscrapers and postindustrial spacecraft are put together with painstaking hand work. Reasonable relationships between design and techniques of production can always be escaped, but the escape entails costs, both economic costs and costs in the real merits of the resulting production.

Any effort to list, categorize and review the qualities of all the materials available and to relate them to appropriate systems of construction and working techniques tends to become an unmanageable survey of questionable usefulness.* That kind of inclusive study will not be attempted here, but it may be useful to focus on one or two issues that arise when an inclusive study is attempted. The distinctions between natural and manmade objects has already been discussed, but in the commonplace classification of materials on the same basis some oversimplifications tend to occur. We tend to speak of such materials as clay, wood or leather as natural in contrast to metals and plastics (and,

*Sir Herbert Read, in *Art and Industry* (Faber and Faber, 1934), undertakes a review of materials of this type of considerable interest and success, although his view is clearly limited to the materials associated with "industrial design" in a narrow sense.

perhaps, glass) as man made, and the latter are often characterized as cold and unsympathetic on this basis. But, bricks and pottery, although made of clay, are quite far removed from the raw material dug from the ground. A tree is not a material; lumber, cut to size and planed or, when made into plywood or particle board, has been extensively manufactured. Metals come from ores dug out of the ground just as clay is dug. Can we really call gold, silver, copper, steel or aluminum artificial materials? Are the chemical processes involved in making plastics from their raw materials different in any inherent way from the processes used to convert trees to lumber or plywood? Are we to consider glass or paper as natural or artificial?

Similar confusions arise when we discuss the meaning of "raw" material. Is lumber a raw or a manufactured material? What of plywood? If iron ore is a raw material, what are pig iron, steel ignot and rolled steel sections? The last are certainly manufactured, but they are nonetheless materials of construction. The complexities of modern industrial production generate hierarchies of materials, interlinked chains of production in which each producer passes its end product on to become the raw material for the next link. Ore is a raw material and pig iron an end product; pig iron is then the raw material which becomes a steel ingot in the next phase of production. Rolled steel sections are an end product at the mill, but become raw material at the fabricating shop where they are cut and drilled, and, at still another level, when they arrive at a building site or at a shipyard ready to be built into a complex structure. This alternation of role between material and product is characteristic of the complex level of technology that we have reached. Simple end products of preindustrial society went from material to product in one or, at most, a few steps in the hands of one producer. Clay became a finished pot, wool from the sheep, a finished garment in a few comprehensible steps that one person could learn to master. The final manufacture of a modern, technological product is a matter of assembly. A ship, an automobile or a building is made by putting together parts, steel beams, nuts and bolts, locks and latches, frames and glass inserts, pumps and motors—any number of manufactured parts that were end products to their makers. In these terms, the modern designer is oddly constrained; he does not deal with an end result that he can have synthesized from raw materials, but with ready-mades that must be organized into a totality that will still in some way express his own intention, not merely as the inevitable result of putting together what already exists. His catalog library is his most vital resource.

86

A by-product of this situation is the need to design components that are destined to become parts of other things. Industrial designers quite often accept assignments such as the design of doors, or windows, faucets or wash basins, wall papers or floor tiles. The question of what is material and what is end product becomes increasingly murky in such situations. Wall papers, floor tile, carpets and furniture are, in a way, end products, but they are also intended to become parts of spaces that will in turn become parts of buildings. What are, for example, the palette of materials of the town planner or the landscape architect? Roads, trees, buildings, streams and ponds, electric poles, fire alarm boxes, no-parking signs, advertising signs—all of these things can be seen as final results, fabricated from parts which have in their turn been fabricated from materials. They can also be seen as materials from which larger totalities can be assembled. In an endless series of nested boxes, the container and the things contained change their role according to the particular box open at the time. In just the same way, material and product have potentially alternating roles, according to the level of conceptualization we bring to bear on the situation.

Craft, process, workmanship and technology are all words describing relationships between material and product. Design success is dependent on managing these relationships successfully. A solution that is conceptually sound can become an unsatisfactory object, through poor selection of materials and constructive techniques. No conceivable level of excellence in manufacturing or construction can, however, make an object serviceable if it suffers from fundamental inadequacies in functional conception. A badly planned building, even if well built of the best materials, will still be a bad building.

Sound selection of material and structural technique, then, joins successful functional solutions to problems as a necessary requirement of any design success. These two closely interlinked activities might be thought to encompass the entire basis of design excellence. Certainly things that work well and are well made are already well ahead of the vast majority of the artifacts that make up the modern world. But there is another dimension that requires discussion.

Meaning in Design

The solution of functional problems through suitable use of materials and constructive techniques is widely accepted as the rational basis for all human activities that involve making things. The average person's common sense supports the ideas that things should do what they are meant to, and that things should be well made, even when, in the exercise of irrational preferences, he fails to act on this basis himself. The technological professions, particularly engineering, accept these criteria and, as discussed earlier, often produce exceptionally excellent designs on that basis alone. While it may be difficult to find agreement about every detail of a particular design in functional and constructional terms, success and failure in these terms are sufficiently understood to give a clear conception of better and worse as general directions. A thing that does not work at all (an airplane that will not fly, a chair that cannot be sat in, a house that leaks and cracks, a shoe that disintegrates in the rain) is so obvious as to make it easy for anyone to understand a value scale on which functional and constructional merit can be measured. Laboratory tests can be used to evaluate less obvious qualities and to make judgments of merit fairly precise in many cases.

Yet, there is a common understanding that something more needs attention—something beyond function and structure. Vitruvius called this something beauty and that would probably be, even now, the most usual way of describing what it is beyond the performance and structural integrity that we seek in the objects we make. We notice that a chair, perhaps, is comfortable and sturdy but, we add, it is ugly. In everyday practice we are constantly distressed to find that satisfactory objects in utilitarian terms—the ones that consumer research organizations rate as best—are seldom those we would choose as well designed. While we can find outstanding examples of pure engineering that exemplify design excellence, others, equally functional, economic and structurally sound, are missing some extra quality that would make us willing to call them beautiful. Although it is tempting to call this extra quality beauty, as Vitruvius did, the term turns out to be somewhat unhelpful. If the terms ugly and beautiful designated understandable and universally recognizable qualities, such as workable and unworkable, or well made and badly made, this might serve us quite well. But in all our efforts to define beauty in any useful way, we find ourselves defeated.

We can easily observe, for example, that what is thought to be beautiful varies greatly with time and place. As recently as the Victorian era, for example, accepted standards of beauty were so different from our current ideas that we find the typical Victorian room, house, or object laughable and quaint but, by present standards, shockingly ugly. Curiously, the things Victorians thought *most* beautiful are the ones of the era we now like least, while other strictly utilitarian and therefore,

The ideal Victorian interior contained examples of almost everything that the occupants owned.

to the Victorian, unaesthetic, objects, such as machinery or engineering structures, are the things we can most admire. The aesthetic ideals of traditional Japanese culture are entirely different from those of the contemporary Western middle class. In our own culture, the preferences of critics and museum directors, whom we might assume know the most, are totally at odds with those of average people. Most of us will even have to admit that our own standards and preferences have undergone changes over the years, and that further changes are quite possible as time goes on. These observations bring into doubt all theories that suggest that there is some absolute and measurable standard of beauty to which we can ask designers to conform.

Certain irritating clichés that one hears endlessly repeated embody some recognition of this problem. "Things are beautiful," one is told again and again, "when they are pleasing to the eye." What does this mean? How does one know if the eye has been pleased, and how can one be sure that whatever pleasurable reaction is felt does not come from some other source? We are pleased by familiar objects that have pleasant associations (with home and childhood, if those things happened to be pleasant), things that our teachers have taught us to like, or for which we have developed a taste from our reading, from advertising and television. How else can we explain that such different things have pleased the eye of people at different times and that even our own tastes can change so quickly? Beauty is in the eye of the beholder, the next cliché tells us. In other words, it is not a real quality of objects, but a kind of reaction on the part of the onlooker. When we say, "That is beautiful," we really mean, "I am having a pleasant reaction"—as much a fact about the speaker as about the object in question.

Over the years, considerable effort been put into attempts to set up reliable ways to build aesthetic quality into the design process. Systems of rules about symmetry, balance, proportion and color have been devised again and again from ancient Egyptian times to the present, yet we remain at a loss to find a trustworthy formula or conceptual framework that can make beautiful as universally comprehensible a concept as workable.* Indeed, the effort is doomed to failure because it attempts to give absolute value to a relative concept. If "it is beautiful" means, in the end, no more than "I like it," the question, "What is beautiful?" must be translated into the question, "What do I like?" This is a route

*This is not to deny the usefulness of many systems of geometric or mathematical control, systems of color harmony and similar kinds or organization of physical realities in the service of design. The point is simply that all of these are tools, possibly useful but not in themselves capable of generating any particular excellence.

that can lead rapidly to the fallacy of majority rule in aesthetics, discussed earlier. One cannot imagine the temples of ancient Greece or the medieval cathedrals being derived from popular opinion surveys conducted in the streets of Athens or Chartres.

And yet, when Sir Henry Wotton transmuted Vitruvius's third value from "beauty" to "delight," he was on the track of something real. Delight is, after all, not a quality of an object, but a reaction of an onlooker. He was suggesting to us that this third value *is* relative, or rather, relational, a matter of the interaction between the thing and the person who encounters it. Delight is a much better term than beauty, because it leads us to think more deeply about the nature of this quality, leaving the door open to the very real possibility that one might delight in something that is not beautiful in any recognized or standardized way. To pursue this matter seriously, we must look more carefully at the beholder. The relationship between the beholder and the object beheld is, in practical terms, easy enough to define. We expect objects to give us some life advantage—something to aid us in the difficult and problematic matter of spending a lifetime on earth. In basic biological terms, we seek in objects aids to survival—survival of the individual and of the species. Many basic things, such as shelter, agricultural implements and weapons have obvious relationships to this need; the more elaborate trappings of advanced civilization may not at first appear to have such basic value, but, insofar as they have value at all, they are all in some way supportive of this fundamental need.

We also know that the extraordinary advantage or ascendancy developed by our species is largely the result of the human ability to find solutions to problems—many of which are ultimately embodied in objects. Human beings are not, after all, as strong as lions or tigers, not as well insulated as polar bears, as numerous as roaches or as well organized as bees; yet we assert our superiority which is to some extent demonstrated in our ability to adapt to every situation and constantly expand our advantage over other species, making human life different in quality from any other form of life known to us. Our primary adaptive tool in this process is, of course, superior brain power, but the brain is only a tool for the processing of information, collected for us through the senses. It is impossible to conceive of thought without presupposing data collected by direct observation and the complex systems which permit us to store and pass on data by indirect means. Words and pictures extend our ability to take in data, but their usefulness is based on a layer of basic information acquired by direct experience. Direct experience, as we know it through our senses, remains our vital link with reality and an essential device for managing our lives. We find our way about, recognize our family and friends, prepare and eat our meals and generally conduct our lives through the information that comes to us by our senses. The brain processes this data and helps us convert it to appropriate action, but the incoming information is vital to this process. When a person is unconscious or in a coma, we often say he has become "like a vegetable," which we recognize to be less than living as we understand it, even if breathing and heart beat are maintained. An event that occurs when one is unconscious (as in sleep) has not really occurred at all, as far as any direct sense of its reality is concerned.

Our relation to reality is, then, a rather peculiar one, by no means as simple as common sense suggests. A real event or situation of which we know nothing does not exist for us. A fictitious reality, presented to us with strong mental impact, can be very real. The experience of reality is necessarily instantaneous—that is to say, it must occur in the present, a time of no duration. There is no experience at the traveling point we call "now"; instead our experience is always one of either anticipation or memory. What we think we know as reality is instead a mental model, built up in memory (or imagination), of data supplied to us by our senses. We all hold in mind an endless stock of images of reality, mental equivalencies that we can refer to and use, even when the realities they purport to represent are not available. To some degree this describes our relationship to things. Our house may keep off the rain and help to keep us warm, our car may transport us about, but the mental reality of each extends far beyond the functional reality.

What we cannot hold in mind or give meaning or value to is best described as chaos, randomness, a total lack of pattern or form. We look at the night sky and see, at first glance, a random arrangement of stars. But we resist that incomprehensible randomness and seek out, in defense, the stars that seem brighter, and soon patterns emerge that we can name and even identify with images of a dipper, a chair or a hunter wearing a sword in his belt. We have thus suddenly transformed randomness and chaos into a memorable pattern that we can carry about and refer to in future. We also carry about powerful mental images of things we have never seen—the form of the earth; our country or state as it appears on a map; the image of the Capitol, the Parthenon, the face of Shakespeare or George Washington. We may have seen one or two of these things; we cannot have seen some of the others; yet they are as strong and specific as many of the things we have seen.

92

The aspect of design that is relevant here involves consideration of this human need to convert the confusion of outer reality into sets of inner equivalents that will be memorable, identifiable and therefore usable in the mental model of reality through which we experience life, make our decisions and plan our future actions.

When we are looking at the sky, at people, at the natural world around us, we use our senses to build this mental model in a way that served us through all of biological evolutionary time. We, along with the other animals more or less similar to us, are built to understand through sensory intake, and to adapt for survival through the mental processing of this intake. The issue that is of interest to us here has to do with the fact that when we make *things,* since we do so with conscious intent, not through simple instinct, we embody in those things the forms that will be the intake of whoever comes upon them. The same processes that we bring to the observation, memory and understanding of, let us say a seashell, come to the observation of a cathedral, an automobile or an egg beater. In the first case the object is a creation of natural evolutionary processes which are, by their very nature, always "right"; in the latter cases, the objects are of human creation and what we observe results from the actions of those who made the thing in question. As viewers and users of the manmade object, we do not change our whole approach to understanding; instead, the senses and mind work just as they would in the presence of a natural object to gather information and conceptualize it in a way suited to thought, understanding and memory.

As long as we consider this process in relation to the natural world, we are discussing a one-way process. Sky, rocks and trees are simply there, their appearance formed without consideration for human requirements. We collect data from them, but they have no active role in offering that data to us. Even animal life, although it may, in the case of the so-called higher species, take on a behavioral relationship with man, does not include any active participation of a conscious sort in designing things for human viewing. It is hardly possible to credit spiders, ants, wasps or beavers with awareness of our visual attention to their constructions.

When a human being makes or builds something, the situation is strikingly different. The maker or builder constantly monitors his own creative work with his eyes and other senses, using self-criticism to refine and improve what is being done. Knowing that others will be seeing, using and criticizing also, the designer cannot escape the awareness that he is involved in a two-way system. The user-viewer will be focusing sensory and mental attention on the completed work in order to understand it, but the designer who makes it is creating the sensory *output* that users and viewers will be taking up. These two situations might be diagrammed thus:

observation of natural object:

observation of manmade object:

In the second case this diagram is still only a partial picture. We must remember that the designer in the process of designing and making his product had to conceptualize mentally what was to be done before actually doing it. That is to say, the idea or ideas preceded realization. The form of the physical object is, thus, in a certain way, a representation of an idea or a group of ideas. If we include this reality in our diagram, it becomes:

94

This turns out to be a diagram of a communication system, as defined by the theorists who, in working to improve telephone and radio communication, have been led to basic generalizations about all such systems. All communication systems have as their purpose the conveyance of message or meaning from one human mind to another (or to many others). The concepts of message, meaning or idea serve to describe the heart of all such process. A message without meaning, without ideas, has no content—it is pointless and worthless and there is no value in transmitting it. A message can, of course, carry meaning which is false or misleading. Modern life is full of such communications; they are the essence of propaganda, political oratory and advertising and we recognize that such messages, unless they are unmasked and devalued, can be destructive to human interests. The "double-speak" of Orwell's 1984 is recognizable to us as capable of bringing about total destruction of meaningful human thought and, in this way, undermining the whole basis of the human species' primary survival techniques—that is to say, the techniques of understanding and thought as the precursor of adaptive action. That we confront so much "double-speak" in contemporary life is ominous, but would be more ominous if we did not have as much ability as we do in a free society to unmask it and seek out the underlying reality.

If this discussion seems to have moved away from design matters, it may be helpful to trace a similar path in design-related terms. A designer (who may also be an inventor or an engineer) conceives an idea for something that will serve some useful purpose. The abstract idea only becomes useful when it is embodied in a real object—a *thing* with physical substance—and in the process of making this object, many decisions will have to be made about its form. While these decisions will be constrained by the object's intended function, they are never in all respects absolutely dictated by functional considerations. A wheel must be round in order to roll, but, within this limit, can take any number of forms, among which the designer must make his decision. As he does so, the forms he develops will become visible and may impact the other senses as well. As long as the object survives, its form will be visible to anyone who cares to look, including future, unborn generations and those who may see the object from a distance via physically or electronically transmitted media.

In this communication system, the message is the designer's idea or ideas about the thing he is designing. These ideas come to be expressed through the forms he chooses, which become a reality that can be sensed by others. As they encounter the object, observe it, use and study it, so the ideas that its form embodies become ideas in the mind of the viewer-user. It is as much a system of communication as language, print or television.

There is a distinction, however, between the communication involved in design and the kind of communication represented by language and the arts (painting, sculpture and music*). When they speak or write or create their works by whatever means, the user of language and the creative artist have as their primary intention the desire to communicate. The sound of language may fill some other secondary purpose (provide background noise in a restaurant, let us say), but the intention of the individual speaker is to be heard and to convey meaning in the process. A painting may decorate a room, music may supply rhythm for dancing; but the painter or composer, insofar as he is truly creative, focuses on communicating ideas and will see these functional uses of his work as secondary and, possibly, even objectionable. One cannot speak or undertake any artistic work without being aware that communication is central to what is being done.

A designer, on the other hand, can quite easily ignore the communicative aspect of what he is doing and focus solely on mechanical function. The attitude expressed in such phrases as "I don't care what it looks like, I am only interested in making it work"—favorite expressions of engineers and other technical people—express this attitude very clearly. The designer, inventor or engineer who takes this position ignores the reality that his product *will* communicate visually, whether he desires it or not. It is a situation somewhat like the "body language" that behaviorists discuss; we can pretend that our body movements have no meaning and are only for practical needs, but they will communicate nonetheless. Similarly, form will communicate, irrespective of its maker's desires, because the human sensory system never stops searching out the meaning discoverable in any reality.

The vernacular and technological designs, discussed earlier, often achieve surprising excellence through forms that turn out to be full of communicative meaning, despite their designers' avowed lack of concern for this dimension. A good craftsman, an expert technician, a skillful engineer is not prevented from arriving at meaningful forms simply because he lacks training in art and does not label himself a designer.

*Architecture, usually included in this list of the major fine arts is omitted here because, in the context of this discussion, it comes closer to the characteristics of design activity rather than art.

His understanding of his work, and his intuitions about what is right, can quite possibly lead him to designs of outstanding excellence. This is particularly true in a field of activity that has a powerful tradition and is fairly narrow in scope. The craftsman-builder of barns or the engineer who designs bridges, through long concentration-in a particular field of work, may develop a remarkable sensitivity in that field. It is a sensitivity that may not be easily transferable—the barn builder might not do so well with the design of table silver, the engineer may be totally inept when he turns his hand to interior design in his own home.

The vernacular and the technological designer are also quite capable of producing products that have no particular merit. A failure to find meaningful form, the deliberate introduction of meaningless form, is entirely possible and, in fact, quite common in these areas. Our admiration of the successes that occur, almost without intention, should not make us blind to the failures that are equally, or possibly more, common.

Success and failure are also common to the professed designer, trained in a design specialty, with strong connections with the world of art, and with the developed, self-conscious intention of producing objects of design merit. Intentions do not guarantee success, of course. Good intentions stand behind any number of efforts in which a superficial grasp of the nature of visual communication has led to the repetition of empty clichés. A church may be clothed in feeble re-creations of Gothic design, for example, in a belief that Gothic detail communicates religiosity in some trustworthy way. A false fireplace of false brick may be introduced into a house in an effort to communicate hominess and similar domestic charms. The intentions behind these shams do not in any way condone the emptiness of the sham. As with white lies, the good intention cannot make a virtue of falsehood.

Taken together, good intentions in regard to communicable purpose, and honesty in choice of form make a better basis for design excellence, but even that combination cannot eliminate the possibility of ineptitude creeping into some stage in the process and limiting the success of the finished product. A comparison with language may clarify some of these distinctions. If we suppose that an event of some import, such as a riot, a battle, or a natural disaster, has taken place, a report can be made in words and communicated to those who were not present. Communication of this kind can have immediate or long-range usefulness in serving human knowledge. But a report of a news event of this sort might, for one reason or another, be entirely false. False reporting is a key device for the manipulation of opinion and resulting human reactions. We tend to condemn false reporting as a form of lying, knowing that, if it is allowed to go uncorrected, it can lead to destructive actions based on faulty knowledge of reality. On the other hand, the report of the event in question may be quite honest, entirely without intention to deceive, but may be so confused and inept as to misinform or blunt the understanding of the recipient. This description might well apply to a large proportion of the everyday news reporting to which we are all exposed.

Truly admirable communication demands complete factual accuracy, as well as clarity in organization and presentation. When writing has these qualities, it becomes literature and we are quite ready to grant that this is an art. When faced by communicative art at its best, we are often ready to ignore or minimize the importance of the detailed, factual content. When reading or watching Shakespeare's *Henry V,* it is not important to us to know whether each documentary fact is correct. We accept the idea that the play embodies an absolutely genuine, larger truth, and we are moved by the skill with which this larger truth is reduced to words and made accessible to our understanding and to our emotions—in a way that more specific everyday realities may not be.

Lest this comparison seem too far-fetched, it might be useful to tie it to a hypothetical design example. Consider as a typical project the design of a single-family house. Functional needs should lead to a rational plan, while knowledge of materials and constructive methods can provide a sound construction program. The house as built will, however, not only offer a shelter of some substance to its occupants; it will also offer a mental image which, so long as the physical reality meets some minimal standard, may be more important to its occupants, visitors and passers-by than the functioning object. But, at its designer's whim, this real house may also become a gross distortion of reality. It can be loaded with mass-produced colonial woodwork, simulated brick and asphalt shingle, equipped with nonworking shutters that would fail to cover the windows even if they did work, equipped with false fireplaces and generally made into a kind of stage set in which myths totally obscure reality. Although this is a description of a very badly designed house, it is easy enough to find actual examples of this level of distortion. The very same house plan and construction program could, it is true, be built without the veneer of falsity.

An honest, straightforward builder might put together a house of a certain integrity, but if he has no particular talent in finding expressive form, the chances are that the end product will fail to move us in any very strong way. We might find it acceptable, but dull—without being able to inspire us with a strong image of its particular planning and structural virtues. What we all hope for is the third possibility: the design that is functional and well put together, but can also be seen as a set of visual forms communicating something articulate, comprehensible, memorable and thus admirable about the reality. These are the kinds of qualities that transform the best of design from mere practical solutions to problem into genuine creative art. Wright's Robie house or Mies van der Rohe's Farnsworth house are each, in their own way, a solution to their occupants' practical needs; each solves a constructional problem, but their landmark place in design history goes beyond that.* It is their demonstration of a set of forms that make something more universally symbolic and meaningful of the actual, practical structure that takes them into the realm of art.

The reader can probably readily call up examples in fields other than residential architecture. One can find a chair that serves its purpose but is an absurd melange of meaningless detail, or one that serves its purpose but is merely characterless and dull; but then, one may find a comparable chair that is also powerfully expressive of a set of ideas that moved its designer to embody them within it for every user or viewer to discover. The same exercise could be tried with automobiles, vacuum cleaners or any other imaginable category of objects of modern life. The search for the third example, the truly outstanding design success, may not always be successful in every category. It is possible that there is no vacuum cleaner extant that is truly an outstanding achievement of design skill!

It seems possible that there is some relationship between the emergence of design excellence in any given historical period and the focus of human concerns in that same period. We probably design best the things that we care most about—even when those may be the things that give us most difficulty. Indeed, often those very things that give most difficulty seem to call forth the most distinguished designs. In the Middle Ages the cathedrals represented an effort to build structures that strained the skill and knowledge of the time. Some cathedrals fell, but

* In fact, it is quite possible to take exception to aspects of the functional or constructive aspects of either of these buildings and many other equally famous design successes. The success lies elsewhere.

Robie house by Frank Lloyd Wright.

Farnsworth house by Mies van der Rohe.

those that did not represent a special kind of high point in design thinking. Even now, almost everyone carries a powerful image of Chartres or Notre Dame de Paris, even if he or she has never seen the actual building. Our own era rarely succeeds in producing a church that rises above mediocrity, and most American modern churches are festivals of banality.* The industrial revolution of the nineteenth century produced steam engines, bridges and ships of a quality that, in their own way, rival that of the medieval cathedrals. Our own time has produced aircraft of astonishing design excellence, but only now and then does such excellence find its way to a house, a chair or an automobile. We care, it would seem, about air- and spacecraft, but find the more commonplace things too routine or too easy to call for any exercise of imagination or competence.

Having dismissed the concept of aesthetics as a component in design excellence at the beginning of this section, and having made the case for communication of meaning as the real concern that lies hidden behind this term, it may now be possible to return to an acceptance of the aesthetic element in what we are seeking. The problem with this term is probably primarily semantic—as long as aesthetic is understood to mean only likeable, it will inevitably lead us into absurd, obscure reasons for aesthetic judgments that psychiatrists are better equipped to trace than designers. The horrors offered by gift shops or novelty shops are, no doubt, liked well enough by those who buy them and take them home to display, but to argue that this certifies their aesthetic value seems, on the face of it, impossible. If, however, we are prepared to assign a deeper level to our understanding of the word liking that involves the mental and emotional satisfactions that derive from the awareness of communicated meaning, then this extended definition of aesthetic experience and design purpose turns out not to be in conflict with the traditional idea at all. Great works of art in any medium (literary, poetic, musical, two or three dimensional) are not necessarily pretty, instantly likeable nor immediately accessible to the great majority of people. The kind of aesthetic success that utilitarian design can achieve is no different. It is less involved in communication of ideas and emotions that are primarily personal, more involved in impersonal abstraction (although a personal element is always present as well); but it communicates meaning through the medium of form, which must now be examined and illustrated in some detail.

*The exceptional churches of Alvar Aalto, Le Corbusier or Louis Kahn only emphasize this point by the very extraordinary nature of their excellence.

Communication through Form
5

No one needs to be reminded that language is a means of communication. That communication is possible without the use of verbal language is surely obvious, but in everyday practice we tend to put so much emphasis on words that the alternative possibilities go almost unnoticed. Speech as a means for communicating ideas of great complexity appears to be a uniquely human invention. Its great usefulness and astonishing success have made us verbal people. This is particularly true of those of us who live in modern, industrialized society. Once committed to print, words become easy to distribute, store and recall as needed. Radio and telephone make verbal communication instantaneous in spite of barriers of distance. Industrial production runs on words—the instructions, the reports, the correspondence and the billing.

In the Middle Ages, literacy was an extraordinary skill, but the ideal of universal literacy is now being reached in most developed countries. Workers must read to be efficient on their jobs, consumers must read in order to understand the advertisements promoting consumption. We now have compulsory education centered on verbal skill. Children are permitted to paint and to model clay in school until they become readers; then, arts and crafts are suddenly reduced to a minor role. For the next twelve years or more, education is concerned with words. Mathematics retains a role as a reminder that other conceptual systems exist, but for most people, very little beyond simple "practical arithmetic" ever becomes really familiar. Geometry, the aspect of mathematics most concerned with space and form, is regarded as difficult and is often made optional on that account. When it *is* taught it is reduced to the rote learning of verbally expressed theorems and divorced from the spatial relationships with which it deals. In our educational system, music, another nonverbal system, is also regarded as optional—a recreational activity in no way comparable to reading and writing as a basic life skill. In spite of its minor role in education, however, music survives in our society as the most striking example of a nonverbal system in which form and meaning can still be detected.

It is an interesting experiment for most people to try to carry on the processes of thought without using words. We find, to our surprise, that for most of us, thought is a constant monologue or conversation conducted silently within our minds. It is like an endless radio program in which we describe to ourselves what we see, discuss plans of action, issue instructions to ourselves and generally generate a stream of consciousness in words. If you attempt to turn off that flow of words, a curious block arises. For most people, however, it turns out to be possible to substitute music. One can listen to a wordless tune in the mind and so become involved in musical and wordless thought. Quite unsophisticated people can do this very readily, even if their musical knowledge is restricted to simple popular music in no way representative of high art.

Visual thinking is an unfamiliar concept to most people and the widespread lack of understanding of the visual arts reflects this. Most efforts to teach art appreciation use the self-defeating technique of explaining works of art in words. Every museum feels constrained to supply explanatory notes so that the visitor confronting a painting or sculpture can bypass any effort to think visually and substitute a verbal monologue in place of direct awareness of the work in question. When viewing the representational forms of historic art, viewers are satisfied to accept title and story as explanation. In the case of abstract modern art, when the typical viewer asks, in desperation, "What does it mean?" he is really asking, "What set of words can I substitute for this image?" When words are supplied, however confused they may be and however far from the reality of the object, the viewer is finally silenced, if not satisfied. He has an explanation even if he cannot understand it and so gives up, assuming that his ignorance stands in the way of true understanding.

This overwhelming emphasis on words as the basis for thought leads our generation to become somewhat disconnected from reality, because the direct experience of reality is not, of course, verbal.

If one tries another sort of introspection, an effort to identify what is held in the memory, most people will find that the stock of retained thought is not all verbal by any means. Mixed in with remembered words, phrases, conversations and readings, there is likely to be other material—perhaps the musical material already mentioned—but always a vast quantity of visual material. We find our way about, not by consulting a memorized guidebook written in words, but by remembering how things look. We remember a person, not through a long verbal description, but by recalling looks, sounds, and possibly, feeling. Food and drink is remembered as a composite of taste, smell, and probably appearance too, but not as a cookbook description. Anyone who questions the limited ability of words to convey certain kinds of information might try the following exercises:

> Write down in words the instructions for finding a particular, difficult-to-find place. It will be a long and troublesome list of "turn right a little after the white house on the left" and the like. Now try giving the same information in a sketch map. Last, try giving the same information by leading someone over the route. The verbal technique will immediately be seen as cumbersome and comparatively ineffective.

> Try to tell a third party how to identify a particular person not known to them so that they can be picked out in a crowd. It will prove almost impossible unless that person has some highly extraordinary characteristic or unless a prearranged signal is used. A photograph can solve the problem in a moment, as the wanted posters in the post office prove.

Making this kind of test also exposes another issue concerning the role of time in thought processes. The passage of time, although difficult to explain, is a reality that we all experience. Thought takes place, as does all experience, within a time frame. "Now" simply describes a point where the past meets the future. Words (and music, too) operate very actively within this time base. Words pass in the time required to say, read or think them, and they must go by in proper order to communicate their intended meaning. Once they have passed, they in some sense disappear and, to be experienced again must be repeated in a recurrence of the same unit of time. Places and things also exist within time, but their reality is not primarily modulated against a time base in the way that speech and music are. One can look at a thing for a short time or a long time. A very brief exposure, sometimes virtually instantaneous, can imprint an image in the memory, where it can be referred to in the future. One cannot recall fully a sentence, a poem or a symphony without allotting the necessary "running time" to the recall, and, having "run through" the recall, it again disappears, unless one wishes to spend the time on another repeat. One can recall a face, a painting or an object for instantaneous reference and can hold it in mind for a short time or a long time as desired. Images are not powerfully time related.

Although the experience of some simple objects can be summarized in a single image, more complex objects commonly require a sequence of images for understanding that are usually connected through a kinetic memory of the process of movement that generated them. Time must enter into such experiences, but it is a less dominating factor. In order to experience a place or a building, for example, one must move around and through it in order to build up the connected sequence of mental images that gives the physical experience reality.* One might do this quickly or slowly and in either case, so long as no part of the space has been missed, say that it had been fully experienced. We can run through in memory in a few moments a spatial experience (a visit to a city, for example) that took quite a long time in reality. Moving pictures exploit the possibilities for this kind of time compression very effectively.

All of this adds up to the realization that an intake of information is quite possible without the intervention of words. All five senses are at work on this kind of intake, but the visual sense tends to dominate, and we often use its name to stand for all of the senses. We constantly call design a visual art, and yet, when we say a chair is well designed, we clearly mean that it feels, as well as looks, right. We also mean that it sounds, smells and tastes right, although in the case of a chair, the involvement of these other senses is likely to be minimal or nonexistent. The tactile senses are very much involved in our experience of many objects. Hearing is a factor in some, while smell and taste have only marginal roles, except in such specialized fields as culinary art and perfumery that we do not usually classify as design activities. For the moment, then, it will be convenient to include under the terminology of the visual sense the receptivity of all the senses. How a thing appears can be understood as including how it feels, sounds, or smells.

The person who designs an object can, of course, explain his design in words or supply "program notes" to accompany the thing itself. Critics

*The idea that architecture is an art of space-time, set forth so convincingly in S. Giedion's *Space, Time and Architecture* (Harvard University Press, 1941 and later editions) is based on this observation.

are in the habit of supplying this kind of verbal program even when the designer has chosen to remain silent. We usually find this sort of verbal prompting rather unnecessary. If we can look at an object, study and use it, go inside a building, live in a town, we quickly find that we have the kind of realistic knowledge that no verbal data sheet can possibly give us. In this process, we use a receptivity built up from our experiences of nature and of humanly created objects, a vocabulary of form comprehension that has been extensively studied in scientific terms under the heading perception.* In this way, we can tell whether things are near to us or far away, whether they are large or small, whether flat or curved. We do this by interpreting the visual clues that our vision picks up in the light of an accumulation of experience. Since contemporary education pays little attention to such matters, we learn almost entirely through experience to interpret visual signals of a more subtle kind—signals that have less direct meaning but are no less real than the simple characteristics of size and shape. Signals of this kind are often described as symbols, although the word is perhaps a dangerous one, because of its widely varied connotations.

Examples may be useful at his point. If an object is large, we can visually perceive its size and come to know this as a characteristic of its reality. If the same object is red, we can observe its redness, but we can also bring to that reality certain kinds of interpretation. We may, for example, conclude that it is made of a red material (brick, for example), but we may also simply note that its maker chose to color it red (with paint or dye, perhaps) and we can search our memory for suggestions as to the symbolic meaning of this color. In a narrow context, this might suggest danger, heat, fire or simply some special importance—all possible symbolic interpretations of the color red. But this involves an effort to convert visual meaning back into words. We might better simply note the color red as having a visual meaning without an immediate word equivalent. Another object might have been made symmetrically, suggesting that its two sides are identical and that this situation is in some way useful to its function. We may also look for verbal symbolism, such as formality or importance—qualities sometimes associated with symmetry. Rather than searching for this verbal significance, we can accept the symmetrical reality as a communication from its designer without making the effort to clothe it in nonvisual meaning.

*Rudolph Arnheim's *Art and Visual Perception* (University of California Press, 1971) is a well-known documentation of this line of thought.

We have been noticing and comparing two kinds of visual symbolism, both of which are in constant use, whether we are aware of them or not. The first kind might be called "analog" symbolism—the form stands in an analogous physical relationship to reality. The appearance of largeness represents real physical size; the red color identifies a material that is, in fact, red; symmetry of form conveys symmetry of structure. In any such situation, meaning can be sought without prior learning. One does not need to have studied any code or visual language to know that large size simply identifies itself. That symmetry of form can mean symmetry of structure, function or both is a trifle more subtle, not quite an identity by analogy, but so close as to be self-explanatory. The differing colors of materials (and their textures and other physical characteristics) are an integral part of their substances. The redness of red brick is hardly a symbol; it is a characteristic of physical recognition. On the other hand, when we look for meanings such as danger in red, or formality in symmetry, we are trying to use coded information—meaning conveyed through arbitrary symbols that must be learned through experience and are part of a particular culture in a particular time and place. We all know that red is used as a code symbol for danger in our society, selected for this role, perhaps, because of analog associations with fire and flame, but this meaning is arbitrary. Some other civilization might choose green to symbolize danger and, moved into that context, we could relearn that symbolic meaning. Even in our own use of such symbolism, our uses of symbols can become quite arbitrary. We paint a railing red to suggest danger beyond and to keep people back. But we make an exit sign red to indicate the route to safety, in case of danger. In western civilization black is the color of death, but in China it is white. This level of arbitrary, coded symbolism is not very deep, is learned, and is constantly subject to change. Closer to inevitability, analog symbolism is the means by which more stable and lasting meaning is conveyed.

We use a number of systems of visual communication to deal with various kinds of information more specialized than the realities of physical objects. It may be useful to pay attention to some of these in their bearing on design. The most familiar are techniques for converting verbal communication to visual media, but other systems invented to deal with realities that are difficult to translate into visual terms are also of interest. Systems of writing are the most obvious and most widely used methods of visual communication. Writing is based on a pre-existing spoken language whose medium is sound. Conversion of sound into something visual presents a problem which has no easy, natural solution. There is no visual analog for an invisible sound. The invention of writing has demanded, thus, some complex assumptions, making possible the development of a code that can be learned and understood. Two solutions, each based on a distinct principle, have emerged for dealing with this problem. The abstract idea of going behind the sound of words to the ideas they represent might seem most reasonable, but it is the means least familiar to Western European culture. This is the route of pictographic writing in which an image is made to stand for an idea—possibly a word but also possibly a concept that we express with many words. Simple diagrammatic pictures can be easily drawn to mean "sun," "man," "water," etc. This is, of course, the basis of the characters of written Chinese and of ancient Egyptian hieroglyphics. Unfortunately for the success of an analog system of writing in our culture, pictures must be so conventionalized for ease of writing that ease of recognition vanishes and, more important, the range of verbal concepts is too great to admit of pictorial representation of more than a small number. What picture will serve for "red," for "love" or for "differential equation"?

To solve these problems it becomes necessary to turn to the second route, the route of arbitrary symbolism, in which meaning is assigned to characters without concern for a pictorial relationship between form and meaning. Since the ideas represented by words (and therefore the number of words needed in a developed language) run to such vast numbers, using a distinct character for each becomes very cumbersome. This is the route taken by written Chinese and contributes to the difficulty of learning to read and write that language.* In Western writing, the number of arbitrary symbols has been reduced by symbolizing sounds, of which only a fairly small number are required, rather than ideas. The Egyptians eventually took this route with hieroglyphics, although preserving the use of some concept symbols. The well-known alphabets, Greek, Roman and Cyrillic, and others less known such as the Ogam alphabet used in parts of northern Europe after about 600 A.D., all take this direction—although none is "perfect" in the sense of having a symbol for every sound and only one sound for each syllable. This perfection has been arrived at in the modern phonetic alphabet used in language dictionaries to aid pronunciation, but still not accepted anywhere for general use.

*That Chinese writing is at all possible to learn reflects the fact that it is by no means "pure" in equating symbols and ideas. The characters incorporate many alphabetic elements which aid memory and comprehension.

容林丘之

Chinese ideogram characters.

Egyptian hieroglyphics.

Ogam alphabet.

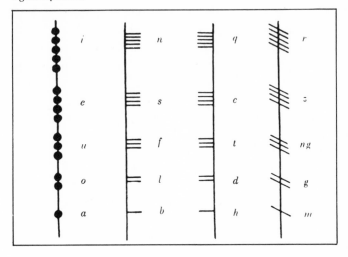

Greek alphabet.

ΑΒΓΔΕΖΗΘΙΚΛΜΝ
ΞΟΠΡΣΤΥΦΧΨΩ

ABCDEFGHIJKLMN
OPQRSTUVWXYZ&.
abcdefghijklmnopqrstuvwxyz

Roman alphabet in a typeface of 1890.

Since alphabetic symbols are in no way analogs for the sounds they represent, alphabets become arbitrary codes that have no meaning until a user receives instruction. Once the code meaning is unavailable, it cannot be rediscovered by any logical means. The well-known story of the role of the Rosetta stone in unlocking the mystery of the lost meaning of Egyptian hieroglyphics is a good illustration of this. Since the design of objects is much more concerned with analogous relationships between form and reality, writing as a system of visual communication leads us away from, rather than toward, the significance of design. In writing, meaning is two steps removed from reality:

Idea (meaning) = word (= sound) = alphabetic symbols

Just as spoken language tends to separate us from the meaning embodied in things and places, written language tends to lead us away from the use of the visual sense for *direct* access to meaning. We search in vain for arbitrary symbols like the letters of the alphabet and, in the process, miss the more direct meaning that form can communicate.

Examination of several other systems of visual communication is useful to us in clarifying these matters and also in demonstrating the superiority of vision in communicating certain kinds of data. Writing is a remarkably satisfactory substitute for speech, but it remains a substitute. An exchange of letters is never as satisfactory as a face-to-face conversation; reading Shakespeare is only a convenient alternative to attending the plays in performance. We value writing for its usefulness in storing meaning and, in modern times, its ease of reproduction, but otherwise it does not *improve* on the spoken work. When the information to be conveyed is not primarily verbal, words, spoken or written, turn out to be less useful than other visual systems.

Consider, for example, the case of music. Without the means to record musical performance, either visually or electronically, a tradition of music is entirely dependent on human memory and the uncertainties of maintained tradition. Ancient music, which covers everything before the early Christian era, is lost to us because no system of notation existed, or at least none has been preserved. The use of words to convey musical composition with any precision is hopelessly cumbersome. Imagine a symphony written down in the form of verbal sentences describing what note to play on what instrument for how long, and it becomes clear how remarkably effective the symbolism of musical notation really is. Like alphabetic writing, it is based on the use of arbitrary symbolism for sounds, although pictorial—that is to say, analog elements—are involved also. Once we accept the notion that tones can be high or low, the placing of symbols above or below a reference line seems a realistic way of representing this aspect of sound. Once we accept the idea that the passage of time will be symbolized by a movement on the page from left to right, placing sounds in relation to a time base becomes possible. Learning to read music requires the learning of a code, just as learning to read words does, but the effectiveness and usefulness of this code is, if anything, even more remarkable. The amazing complexity of a symphonic or operatic performance can be written down, printed, stored on a shelf and pulled out, even after the passage of hundreds of years, and recreated with excellent reliability. Written music is thus in some way closer to the reality it represents than are written words. The written notes represent sound, which has its own (musical) meaning. Written words represent sounds which have a meaning outside themselves. When we write:

the meaning is simply the sound which the reader can play, sing or hear in the mind's ear. When we write the letters C-I-R-C-L-E, we represent the sounded word "circle" which has meaning only if we know that it represents the form: ○ a form which takes many words to define precisely as the dictionary attempts to do.

A more modern and more specialized code is involved in the engineering diagrams for electronic devices called circuit diagrams. As in music, verbal description of the realities of many such inventions would be hopelessly complex. All that matters, as far as the working of the device is concerned, is that certain components be present and that they be interconnected by electrical conductors in a very specific way. The convention that a line will represent interconnection seems so natural that we accept it at once as a picture of reality—almost an analog for the physical fact of a wire or a soldered joint. Arbitrary symbols are needed for the components, but the symbols such as

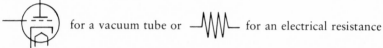 for a vacuum tube or ⟍⟋⟍⟋⟍ for an electrical resistance

come close to being pictorial. Suddenly it becomes possible to give all the information about a radio, a television set or any similar device in one small (even if complex) diagram. Without this communication system, left only with words to give the data, the task of designing, building and maintaining such devices would be vastly more difficult.

Another kind of visual analog communication deserving of special attention is the making of maps. Our experience of life on the surface of the earth involves movement, constrained by the presence of oceans, rivers, mountains and similar geographical features. Walking or riding in more or less straight lines as we do severely limits our ability to build a conceptual understanding of the forms of geography. Making visual diagrams of geographic realities is a very old idea. But, with increasingly sophisticated geometric theories, techniques of surveying, and the modern thirst for data, we are seeing the development of mapping as a tool for making accessible a complex of information, hardly understandable in any other way. However useful the words of a traveler's memoirs or the text of a guidebook, neither can ever really make clear the physical relationships of geography. A map or chart, through the simple analog techniques of size reduction and the use of scale, can put the form of Europe, France, Paris or a particular neighborhood before us on the table in a way that no verbal account can match. A map is not, however, a simple picture. Aerial photographs and the images returned to us from spacecraft have many parallels with maps, but they include too much reality to serve our needs for conceptualization. Water and land may be hard to distinguish in a photograph. Although clouds are also realities, they can obscure the geographic reality. In an aerial photograph, Pennsylvania and New York are not printed in different colors, as they are on a map. The names of cities and towns do not appear in neat print. All of these matters are humanly invented circumstances, quite real to us, that we need in place to make a map communicative. A photograph shows us only physical reality and leaves out political and cultural matters that concern us also.

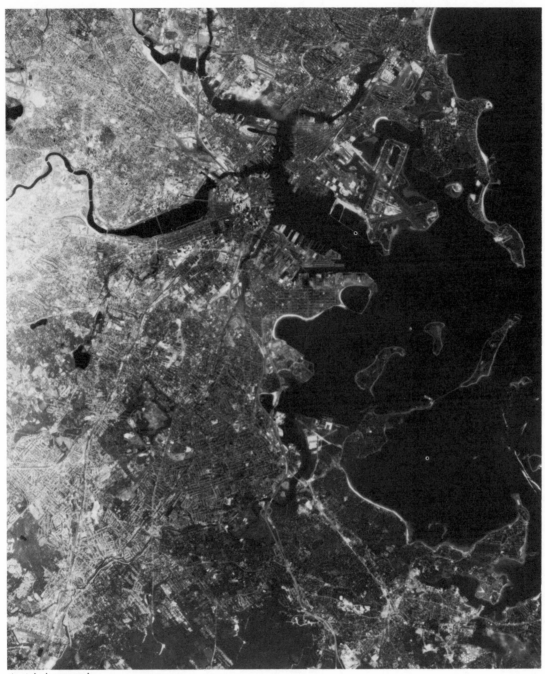

Aerial photograph.

Road map.

Portion of an 1835 map of Florence.

Railway map.

We do not hesitate, as map makers, to jumble together a scaled representation of the geometrics of the earth's surface—the conventions that help us separate out the things that we view as most important (land versus water, for example), the political facts of nations and administrative subdivisions, place names and any other data we may choose to include or omit. A rail map shows railroads very black and omits roads. A road map makes roads red or blue according to the quality of the paving, but omits railroads. A chart for air navigation shows radio navigation aids with great clarity (although they have no solid physical substance and could disappear at the turn of a switch) and reduces roads and railroads both to the point of invisibility. Maps are visual devices for presenting information in a visually manageable form, selected on the basis of the map maker's priorities.

It is interesting to notice how useful and how understandable this half-analog, half-arbitrary system of communication is. Everyone seems able to understand a map, in most cases without any special instruction. Small children will look at a road map and ask, "Where are we? Where are we going?" and understand the answers at once. People with limited education, probably not too well able to deal with complex verbal instructions, can use a subway map to help find an obscure destination. The effectiveness of such a system for making understandable the obscure and the invisible in reality, and in creating a relationship between the arbitrary elements of human communication and the realities of physical space are quite remarkable. We take this for granted as routine.

The relation of all of these systems to the intentions of design is quite close. One might say that the communicative purpose of design is to make of every humanly created thing a map of itself. A plan, a diagram or an actual map can help in the understanding of an artificial circumstance, but when something is truly well designed, the best plan, diagram or map is integral within the object itself. As long as the designer of an object concentrates on the solution of a functional problem and is dealing with the problems of construction, the process is, in a sense the creation of the geography of that object. When attention focuses on the communicative, the expressive (even, if we want to use the term, the aesthetic) aspects of the thing in question, the role changes to that of map maker. The form is itself, its own analog, but the decisions about what to emphasize, what to minimize and what to introduce in the way of arbitrary symbolic elements makes a visually comprehensible image of the raw reality. To retain and use the geographical concepts of North America, Italy or Amsterdam, we need the mental image that a map provides. In the same way the realities of Westminster Abbey, a Model A Ford or "my house" are made accessible to understanding and memory through the form imagery that their designers gave them.

In seeking out parallels with, and differences from, the fields of design, one other area of visual communication requires special attention. This area is, of course, the arts, in particular the visual arts. Painting, sculpture and architecture are usually considered the major visual arts or the fine arts (along with the fourth, nonvisual art of music). It is recognized that each of these arts includes an aspect of design, by which we usually mean the management of abstract form. In the case of architecture, design is clearly the primary and most significant aspect of that art. At the same time, the professions that focus on product or industrial design, interior and graphic design, are also to some extent regarded as arts, albeit minor ones or, as expressed in the Dewey Decimal library catalog system, "useful arts." By implication, the fine arts are thus being classified as useless, a view that most artists are hardly likely to embrace. The position of architecture is particularly curious, since no one can question its focus on the production of useful structures, while its acceptance as a fine art is, at the same time, very firmly established. It is even often called the mother of the arts, although the claim to this title may be somewhat unclear.

Any number of philosophers, theorists and writers have tried to make some sense of the overlapping roles of the various arts through the development of one or another system of orderly classification, comparable to the systems of classification that have served to clarify biological realities. A simple classification based on materials used comes first to mind. A painter uses paint, a sculptor, clay, stone or bronze, an architect . . . well, the materials of construction. This view of things, while simple and not altogether inaccurate, seems to lead nowhere beyond the obvious. It has been supplanted, therefore, by a more subtle view that suggests that each kind of art has its proper medium—in a sense larger than that of simple material. Thus, music has sound as its medium, and painting (and the related arts of drawings and graphics), two-dimensional, flat space. Sculpture, in contrast, operates in three-dimensional space. Since architecture is also three-dimensional, one must further note that the medium of sculpture is usually solid—that is to say that the interior spaces of sculpture are not normally significant and, in most cases, do not even exist. Architecture's claim to a special role as an art has to do with the fact that its concerns are not limited to three-dimensional mass, but extend to space, the relationships of solid

118

masses and the hollow interior spaces within. S. Giedion's title, *Space, Time and Architecture,* derived from his realization that three-dimensionality is always sculptural and that the special characteristics of architecture have to do with "four-dimensionality," that is, concern with space and time, qualities that modern physics see as intertwined in the space-time continuum. Within such a classification, there is, of course, a considerable degree of overlap between the different arts. Some surface painting with a degree of three-dimensionality, such as bas-relief, is largely two-dimensional, but is still considered sculpture. Some sculpture has internal space and might be called architectural. Some architecture is solid (consider the pyramids of Egypt) *and* sculptural. If a chart attempted to show the relationship between these arts, it might be something like the following:

two dimensional ("flat")	three dimensional ("solid")	four dimensional ("space-time")
painting ———————— — — —		
— — — sculpture ———————— — — —		
— — — architecture ———————		

While this classification puts in order the formal characteristics of these arts, another kind of difference that distinguishes architecture from the other arts (including music and the literary arts) revolves around the word "useful." Except for architecture, our expectations of usefulness in art, of any narrow and practical kind, are quite limited. Painting, it is true, can decorate a room, if one can call that a use. It can be instructive (as in medieval religious painting) or it can be a medium of propaganda—usually with disastrous effect on its value as art. Sculpture can serve parallel functions but, particularly in modern times, it has become clear that such usefulness is purely incidental to the real uses of art, which lie rather in communicating human thought and emotion of a nonfactual, personal sort. In the end, we value Giotto's Arena Chapel frescos, not as a Bible story comic strip, and Michelangelo's *David,* not as a piece of civic decoration, but rather, in each case, for the ability of the work to put us in touch with the character and mind of the artist. Like the medium of paint or stone, the ostensible content or story or illustration is merely a vehicle for a deeper level of communication—a kind of communication that does not translate easily into words because it is truly and deeply visual.

The quality that makes architecture different is, of course, the fact that most buildings have some kind of usefulness as a *primary* purpose. While it is theoretically possible to build buildings that have no purpose except that of visual communication, the great cost, permanence and space requirements of buildings usually preclude this kind of construction. Some monumental structures (triumphal arches or tombs, for example) approach this, but even then there is usually some utility in mind. The pyramids function as tombs, although that use can hardly be said to have justified their size and specific form. Moreover, since architects are rarely in a position to finance their own buildings (in the way that a painter or sculptor can usually finance all but the largest works), their freedom to make them *personally* expressive is somewhat limited. The unique personal character that constitutes the style of an individual painter or sculptor becomes one of the primary values in his work. To be confronted with individual personality in the design of an office building, hotel or a factory can easily appear too personal for a structure used by many varied people over a long period of time. Some buildings can be called "expressionist" by virtue of this kind of dominating, personal character and some such buildings are interesting and effective; consider, for example, Erich Mendelsohn's Einstein Tower observatory. But we tend to pull away from such individualism in building, realizing that the personal and unique is only appropriate to exceptional structures differentiated from a background of the great majority of more impersonal buildings. Buildings are needed in such numbers and crowded together so closely in towns and cities that the thought of making every building powerfully and uniquely personal suggests the possibility of chaos.* This does not preclude the development of individual and personal style in architecture. Even the reserved and seemingly impersonal buildings of Mies van der Rohe turn out to be quite individualistic; as the weakness of imitations illustrates, it is simply that here the expression is more concerned with the structure itself, its uses and its materials than with the private and personal emotions of the architect.

Competent painting or sculpture is expressive of its own medium, but without other expressive content is hardly worth producing. Architecture that can be described in parallel terms may well be extremely useful and is often preferable to an excess of misplaced personal expression. Much of the eighteenth-century architecture of modest buildings, even

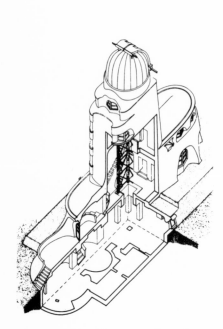

Einstein Tower observatory design by Erich Mendelsohn.

---

*The personal and often eccentric buildings built at world's fairs offer a demonstration of what this possibility can mean.

whole areas of cities, can be described in this way, and we admire and enjoy surviving examples very much. If architecture had no possibility of transcending this kind of technical competence, it would be reasonable to ask whether it should be considered an art at all. But it does have this transcendent capacity, both in the individualistic, expressive kind of building and in the less personal kind of architecture. Anyone who has taken the trouble to notice will remember experiences of approaching or entering buildings that generated a deep and emotionally moving sort of response. Some of the great medieval cathedrals (Chartres, for example) have this kind of power, but so do many less obviously monumental spaces: a simple room in an American Shaker community dwelling, for example, or the reading rooms in either of Labrouste's great Paris libraries of the nineteenth century.* The first two examples are highly impersonal in character, using a style that had a long history of usefulness in the hands of many different architects and craftsmen. Labrouste's work is unique, but its character is not personal in the sense of being expressive of his private attitudes and emotions. The best of modern architecture (Le Corbusier, Aalto, Mies van der Rohe) offers this delicate balance between the production of spaces that have a personal impact, and a certain restraint which limits the intrusion of the personal aspect of what we call personality. Expression and emotion can be present, but they are realized in a way that has a degree of universality so that we do not feel the individual intruding his private views in an inappropriate, public context.

This discussion of architecture as an art provides a prototype for understanding the status of the other design professions—from the scale of landscape and town planning to that of products and other artifacts. In practice, the design of many elements of our world is carried out by people who make no claim to any concern with the arts. Nevertheless, their success is governed by the degree to which they find their way to an understanding of the communicative elements of form, whether or not they choose to apply the term art to their work. We also have a group of professions trained, for the most part, in art schools, where it is generally agreed that an element of art is important. Landscape architects, industrial designers, interior designers, graphic, advertising and fashion designers are examples of these art-oriented professions. Although tradition does not give them the status of fine art accorded to architecture, there are very strong parallels that help to clarify their roles.

*Bibliothèque Sainte-Geneviève (1843–50) and Bibliothèque Nationale (1858–68).

Cathedral of Chartres.

Reading room of the Bibliothèque Nationale by Henri Labrouste.

*Interior of American Shaker colony dwelling at
Sabathday Lake, Maine.*

Since the work of each of these professions generally has a large public, population of users or consumers, the role of the designer takes on an impersonal quality. An artist can paint a painting in solitude for his own satisfaction and feel content even if he communicates with one viewer, living or in some distant future. The architect is more often concerned with some population of user-occupants who must, at least, find his building serviceable. The designers of these other professions have, if anything, even less scope for intimate personal expression. Any object can take on unique qualities of meaning as a result of the form given it by its designer, and yet we resist as absurd the idea of a deep-freeze unit or snowmobile as a medium for serious communication of personal and emotional significance. Instead, our search for visual communication is limited to the realities of function and structure which, if met with clarity and competence, can be moving in some more impersonal way.

Both in architecture and in the other design fields, a kind of natural language of form exists which appears to be based in our knowledge of nature and our awareness of physical phenomena. When we see a large mass, we conclude that the object in question *is* in fact large; the arrangement of its parts in a horizontal line or a vertical stack leads us to conclusions about the spatial relationship of those parts. Symmetry, or the lack of it, leads us to conclusions about spatial and structural organization of another kind. In much the same way, we can understand something about materials and structure from visual clues. Mass has a different appearance from framing. A power saw makes a cut of a different kind than a hand chisel. Casting and molding lead to shapes different from those generic to cutting, carving or assembly of separate parts. Wood has appearance characteristics different from those of metal, glass or leather. All of this seems so obvious and mundane that it should hardly need mention, and yet, we are surrounded with objects whose designers, usually in pursuit of some commercial goals, have taken opposite directions. A compact object is deliberately made to seem larger than it is through distortions of form; metal or plastic simulate wood; real relationships between parts are concealed or minimized, while spurious relationships are invented and dramatized. Any visual relationship that a viewer or user may form with such objects will turn out to be false and, ultimately, disappointing.

*The architectural competitions in which many architects submit designs for the same project are an interesting demonstration. A number of excellent solutions are usually entered and juries often have difficulty in deciding which is best among a number of outstanding proposals that may be totally different.

In contrast, the visual relationship with objects that express their functional and constructive realities in a strong and articulate way turns out to be lasting and rewarding. Any fear that this kind of emphasis on relationship with reality leads to dullness and monotony is entirely unfounded. Each designer discovers an infinity of choices in deciding how to deal with a particular functional problem and in creating a visual expression for that solution. Given identical programs, no two architects would conceivably arrive at identical or even closely similar designs for a building.* There is no one visual treatment that is exclusively characteristic of a particular metal. This explains why there can still be a powerful personal element in seemingly impersonal design. As a particular designer works on a problem, he must make his own judgments about the relative importance of different aspects of the thing he is designing—assign priorities to conflicting values and find ways to bring unrelated elements into some coherence. He must choose the specific visual, symbolic means that will, in his view, best communicate his purposes to the awareness and satisfaction of the user.

There is nothing inherent in the nature of design as art that precludes the addition of elements for purely visual reasons. Modern theory has run into considerable trouble over this issue. Most humanly created objects include extra visual elements that we usually call decorative. A Greek temple is surrounded by columns creating a portico that has no clear usefulness, decorated with carved stone details imitative of wood construction. The painted patterns on American Indian pottery have no strict utility nor do stripes or flowers woven into the textiles or printed on the wallpapers of the eighteenth and nineteenth centuries. Why are we so willing to accept these decorative additions and so critical of the false shutters on a modern suburban house or the chrome tail-fins added to automobiles?

The issue relates, once again, to meaning. Decoration appears in any number of historical contexts where, at its best, its role is always to emphasize, to clarify and to intensify visual comprehension. The Greek temple has only a most minimal function, in any practical sense. It is, rather, a ceremonial object of primarily sculptural character. Its basic form and its decoration are all products of a long tradition focused on the development of a symbolic object to dramatize that tradition. Seen in its own proper landscape and light, it can be very moving. When removed from context and turned to other uses (as happened in the Greek revivals of the nineteenth century), the same forms complete with the appropriate decorative detail, are not at all the same. A modern Greek-temple museum or skyscraper are curiosities, not powerfully beautiful in any sense. The patterns on American Indian pottery sustain traditions of deep significance, reveal the craftsmanship of the maker, and, in addition, help to reveal the form of the pots by placing on their surface patterns that emphasize the three-dimensional form the potter has made. Decoration has a role in design whenever it serves these purposes of helping to reveal form, demonstrate the role of craftsmanship in the production of the object, or explicate historical and traditional symbolic meanings. At its best, decoration of objects acts as a kind of visual running commentary on the realities beneath.

Why, then, do we find decoration in such bad repute in modern contexts? We have broken off the traditions underlying most decorative systems, without developing any alternative vocabularies. Most historic decoration is deeply involved in traditions of craftsmanship. Primitive decorative systems have both craftsmanly and mystical meanings for their makers and users. Industrialization suddenly made it easy to add complex decoration cheaply and, as a result, set loose a glut of decoration, formerly only available at great cost. What was meaningful when hand carved as part of the mystic value of a Greek temple becomes something else when mass produced in castings at an iron foundry. The carving of fine handmade furniture becomes debased by the routine of mass production and even more debased when reproduced in molded plastic. It is not only the elimination of craftsmanship that is involved; we have also separated design from the processes of production. When a hand-weaver invents, or elects to use, patterns learned as part of his craft, those patterns may well turn out to be communicative and meaningful. When a designer makes patterns on paper, with no connection with textiles or loom, and simply directs that the power loom should turn them out in substantial quantity, those patterns become mere, pointless fussiness.

In these ways, traditional decoration has been changed into something that can be carelessly introduced into any and every situation. The goods in any mail-order catalog are an index of shoddy imitative decoration, laid indiscriminately over every available surface, serving, more often than not, to conceal defects and distract, through some intimation of prettiness, from the shoddiness of the underlying object. Successful modern decoration has been developed by a number of designers (one thinks of Horta, Guimard, Gaudi, Sullivan and Wright), but it demands individual craftsmanship, just as historic decoration did. Wherever production becomes impersonal, involving an assembly line or mechanical reproduction of a standard model, the meaning of decoration comes into question. The designer finds it necessary to turn instead to the decorative qualities inherent in the color and texture of various materials and finishes.

In this context, the role of color becomes particularly significant. The natural colors of materials seem always right, communicating some sense of the qualities of their intrinsic nature. But more and more modern materials have no natural color or require a protective layer that has no color characteristic of its own. What is the natural color of plastic? In most cases a color additive is needed if the material is to have any reasonably consistent color characteristic at all. This can be *any* color desired. Many metals require a surface coating as a protection against oxidation—and this paint coating can as well be one color as another. To speak of the natural color of, for example, an automobile, makes no sense. Parts that need to be chrome plated for protection will have a characteristic gleam, but other metal surfaces can be painted in any color. It is customary in situations of this kind to offer to users a choice of a variety of colors, somewhat arbitrarily chosen. Yet, we gravitate toward certain colors for certain uses in some kind of recognition of the meaning that color can communicate. Bathroom fixtures, for example, are most often white, partly because this is a natural color for porcelain, partly because, since white exposes any trace of dirt, it appears to us as sanitary, and partly for reasons that are expressive or communicative of function. Bathroom fixtures are made, of course, in a great variety of colors, but colors other than white are usually restricted to decorative uses where the role of the fixtures in some total concept outweighs the significance of the specific color.

Cameras and related equipment are usually finished in black with, perhaps, some metallic trim. From time to time, other colors have been used, but never with any great conviction. Why do we feel so clearly that a camera must be black? The absence of any chromatic color makes black a noncolor and so it becomes the logical color expression for anything that has no logical reason to be of any particular chromatic color. It is thus the color of machinery, equipment, of things regarded as serious. Henry Ford is supposed to have said that his famous Model T was "available in any color as long as it's black." Just as white can be seen as symbolic of cleanliness and sanitation, black can become the color of utility, clarity and seriousness. The bright orange or yellow of road-building equipment, the red of fire-fighting equipment, the green of British racing cars, the yellow of Swiss postal system vehicles, are all communicative and meaningful ways to color the necessary protective coating that must be applied to the natural materials of utility objects.

Many if not most of these systems communicating meaning are rooted in conventions that have only longevity to support their merit. And yet, there stand behind these conventions, and behind the effectiveness of most communication through form, some larger psychological values. For reasons that are not easy to explain, we all have certain common reactions to aspects of form. Red and the colors near it in the spectrum are seen by everyone as hot, active and exciting, while the colors at the green-blue end of the spectrum are quiet, calming or even depressing. Horizontal forms are reposeful; vertical forms, anything from stable to aggressive; and oblique or diagonal forms, active. These are the clichés of books about elementary design, and yet are also observable realities.

Our understanding of consistent and significant reactions to form is, as yet, limited and always subject to the silliness of oversimplification. Nevertheless, we are all still accessible to communication of a very deep psychological nature through form, shape, color, texture. We are drawn to certain things, repelled by others in ways that cannot be easily explained, unless we admit that visual form reaches certain deep levels of the human mind that are only partially understood. The inexplicable power of the works of certain men—those whom we call geniuses—must be the result of their ability to reach, through whatever medium they may choose to work in, these deep and universally meaningful levels. Analysis at a mundane and rational level can help in the understanding of great art, but it does not reach to the level at which the true greatness of the *most* meaningful and communicative art lies. It is only at a deeper level of mental process that we can hope to explain the power of the music of Bach, the paintings of Paul Klee or the architecture of Le Corbusier.

Other
Times and
Places
6

T HE ASSERTION that has been made a number of times in this book
—that civilizations prior to modern industrialization and surviving
"primitive" civilizations have consistently produced design of high
quality—requires the presentation of visual evidence. It is not possible
to undertake a general historical survey here, but it may be useful to
single out for examination a small number of situations which may
themselves suggest other sources of research.

One objection to the search for design excellence in cultures that are
far from us in time, location and attitude is that a process of selection
intervenes, bringing to our attention only those things that are best. Important objects of value are more likely to survive over long periods of
time than everyday, commonplace things—partly because they are usually made better and from more lasting materials, partly because they
are more likely to be valued and preserved by succeeding generations.
And, indeed, when objects are chosen for display in museums and to
illustrate books, it is most often the objects that we now think best that
are singled out. To some extent, this may be a valid caveat, and in our
critical attitudes there may also be a certain element of romanticism and
nostalgia lending an added attraction to the products of remote civilizations. But if we make an effort to seek out representations of the
commonplace to compare with the important, and if we make some
allowance for bias in our views, we are still confronted with real differences in design qualities between modern industrial civilization's
productions and those of these seemingly exotic civilizations. The com-

parison is so unfavorable to our own average achievements that we have reason to consider seriously why we do things so badly.

This disturbing comparison becomes all the more striking when we consider the very small populations that produced the artifacts we are inspecting, and the limitations on availability of materials and technology that applied when these things were designed. In contrast, we now have a vast world population with communications that make available knowledge accessible to all educated people, wherever they may be, and we also have access to materials and techniques and knowledge of underlying scientific principles that free us from the restrictions of earlier civilizations. The benefits of these changes in health, comforts and conveniences are obvious and well known. The reasonable expectation that our physical environment and all the individual objects that constitute it would show a similar improvement has not been fulfilled. Our contentment with the quality of life in modern times has been based on a real improvement in comfort and convenience, but continued improvement is becoming increasingly difficult.

Adequate food, clothing, housing and a work life that does not make excessive demands, plus the luxuries of mobility and access to interesting personal pursuits are now offered to most citizens of developed countries. The expectation that the quality of life should be entirely satisfactory thus seems only reasonable. The discovery that all of these advantages may be compatible with a decline in the quality of life is only surfacing as a paradoxical reality as the full achievements of the industrial revolution come to their fruition.

This paradox has its roots in a variety of situations, but among them we must surely include the fact that, for our own era, we have not developed a means to design a coherent and meaningful environment, complete with all its constituent artifacts, that is comparable to the circumstances of past civilizations.

The solutions to our own problems must begin in a comprehension of what it was that other peoples, so much less well equipped technologically, did so well.

Stonehenge, one of the most spectacular of prehistoric remains. Functionally, it was an observatory, clock, calendar and, perhaps, temple. Its continuing visual aesthetic impact survives with surprising power.

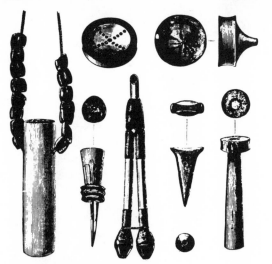

Utilitarian objects from various South American Indian cultures.

African weaving. Patterns are generated by the weaving process and always reflect its mechanical realities.

Nomadic tent village of North American Plains Indians. The tepees were often quite large and the arrangements of adjustable ventilation and smoke outlet flaps were highly functional.

Chinese jade snuff bottle. Simple form exploiting the natural qualities of the material.

The Egyptian pyramids, tombs and also sun-cult objects having complex geometric relationships to astronomical phenomena. The aesthetic impact survives the obsolescence of other significance.

A group of ancient Egyptian artifacts. Clarity of design purpose is never in doubt.

The Greek temple has become a kind of symbol for physical beauty. Its functions were largely symbolic, its aesthetics based on development of obsolete structural techniques into abstract form with complex mathematical geometric bases.

The essence of medieval thought had to do with protection, with defense from a world that had lost any sense of order. The monastery was an oasis of withdrawal from an impossible world. S. Martin de Canigou.

Bodiam Castle, Suffolk. Another form of protection and isolation, the medieval castle.

Nothing suggests the emphasis on defensive protection more strongly than the medieval suit of armor. The fighter best defended would prevail. The functional subtleties are remarkable and the visual impact striking.

Medieval city planning was equally involved with defense. What now appears picturesque in terms of towers, bridges and battlements was in concept strictly purposeful. Carcassonne.

Everyday structures of the Middle Ages survive, here and there, into modern times. Their functional logic makes them still striking in visual terms. Cottages on the Isle of Skye.

Ancient bridges from the time of the
Romans until the advent of modern
engineering are exercises in efficient use of
the compressive strength of stone. The arch
is the key technique for conversion of stony
strength to span of open space.

The gothic cathedral, most obvious of
medieval monuments, is an extension of
the arch into a complex engineering system
for the enclosure of vast spaces. Exeter.

Renaissance concern with use of classical detail tends to obscure the underlying concern
with logic and order for the modern viewer. The Villa Capra (Rotunda) of Palladio at
Vicenza as illustrated in his Four Books of Architecture.

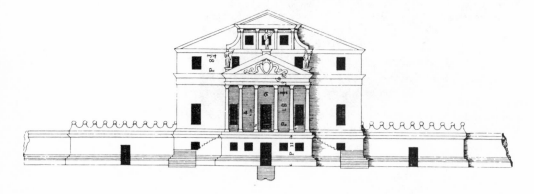

136

The Baroque gardener or landscape architect organized nature in accordance with his systems of geometric logic. Le Notre's gardens at Versailles.

Town planning of the Baroque era. Comparable concern with urban form remains a rarity in modern times. The Piazza del Popólo in Rome.

Musical instruments introduce a special and complex relationship between form and function. Is the form of the violin a result of striving for a desired sound, or is the sound a by-product of an invented form?

*The Royal Crescent, houses of a
speculative real estate development in
Bath.*

*Renaissance order, as a widely accepted
vocabulary of form, becomes a basis for a
visually coherent urban scene. A Georgian
street in London.*

Contemporary
Directions
7

Despite earlier assertions that our own modern era is a time of particularly inept design, it is still possible to find examples of objects and extended situations that suggest the possibility for an acceptably designed environment to be as great now as ever before. It is even possible that there is quantitatively more excellence now present than ever before, but, when viewed in the context of a surrounding glut of thoughtless and shoddy productions, it tends to lose its significance. We make and have more of everything and are ourselves more numerous than has been the case in any previous time in history. As a total population, we have lived through a period of some 150 years of totally uncritical acceptance of anything and everything offering any sort of short-term comfort, convenience, mechanical or economic advantage. As a result we have built an environment that emphasizes quantity above quality in everything.

The emerging dissatisfactions with our situation still do not extend to anything like the total population. Most people like almost everything they have and everything offered them for future consumption. Yet, there is an expanding core of critical evaluation that compares the quality of our physical circumstances very unfavorably with those of the peoples surveyed in the preceding section. When this more discriminating evaluation takes place in the minds of professional designers, we discover a willingness to search for better ways to form things than those of the normal mass production of most consumer products. The term good design has taken on a meaning beyond the dictionary definitions of the two words, to suggest instead a movement, almost a cult, oriented toward change and reform. To design simply to do what may make sense is so unusual and contrary to normal practice as to generate quite active opposition.

The residents of a neighborhood where all of the houses are foolish shams of some historic style will often be outraged by the intrusion of a single, well-designed house. Consumers, accustomed to a flow of annually changed automobile models, each more objectionable than the last, will find a well-designed car disturbingly radical and therefore suspect. Recent design history is an endless succession of anecdotal accounts of the surprising emergence of something sensible, followed by the unpredictable story of rejection or, in some exceptional cases, acceptance.

In the preceding section, a survey was offered, in some rough chronological order, of design excellence in history. This survey might be called a vertical cross section. This section is oriented to our own time (interpreted loosely as the last fifty or sixty years) and involves a similar survey organized horizontally—that is to say, in terms of object types. Just as the last section had no possibility of being inclusive, this section must inevitably be very limited and therefore erratic in its coverage of the vast range of artifacts that make up the physical setting of modern life. The aim has not even been to select only things that are best, but rather to present a cross section that offers a basis for discussion and evaluation of the complex issues involved in the judgment of what is good.

Because of the vast variety and complexity of the things made by modern civilization, even a logical system of object and environment classification becomes difficult. If the organization used here involves some overlaps, contradictions and missing areas, it is in the end not very important to the effort to supply the reader with cases that he can consider for himself to check the rationality of the theoretical ideas offered in earlier chapters. Using space to illustrate offensive examples seems an unattractive way to make points, but in a few cases this has been done in an effort to insure clear distinctions.

Probably no reader will agree with every point made or be able to accept as reasonable every example chosen. Since the issues dealt with here are not matters of absolute and provable fact, there must always be room for a wide range of differing opinion about the better and the best. When the extremes are confronted, those things that are at least better (if not best) are compared with what is worst, and it becomes easy to make clear the directional signals that point toward better and worse. That worse should be the norm of our production, while better remains unusual, rare, strange and even, through unfamiliarity, distressing to so many people is the curious and disturbing characteristic of modern civilization that concerns this book. To offer visual demonstration that excellence is still identifiable, attainable and worth pursuing is the purpose of this section.

A pretechnological vernacular at its best. The sailing ship.

Vernacular traditions in farm and other rural building survive through centuries until displaced by modern technology. Farm buildings in Switzerland.

The most striking manifestation of nineteenth-century technology, the steam locomotive. The typical American locomotive (4–4–0) as built by the Grant Locomotive Works of Paterson, New Jersey.

The sailing ship vernacular gives way to steam technology. The City of Rome, *a much-admired liner of 1881.*

No. 6324A.

Modern technology has its basis in the logic of science. Conversion of scientific concept into technological reality depends on the instruments of exploration and of measurement. A surveyor's theodolite.

The realities of steel construction were only very gradually allowed to become visible in buildings. McKim Mead and White's New York Pennsylvania Station was Roman everywhere but in the actual train shed where steel construction became visible.

CONTEMPORARY DIRECTIONS

143

The modern highway is a particularly characteristic aspect of the contemporary, automotive world. In excess, it has become a threat; only rarely is it planned to embody and conserve the existing landscape's qualities. The Taconic Parkway, New York State.

Visually, even the sprawling engineering of the highway interchange can be expressive when seen from a suitable viewpoint.

Modern structural engineering at its most expressive. The Salginatobel bridge of Robert Maillart, 1929–30. Maillart's bridges were regarded as ugly by governmental authorities in Switzerland at the time when they were proposed, and so were usually considered only in obscure locations where they would be little seen.

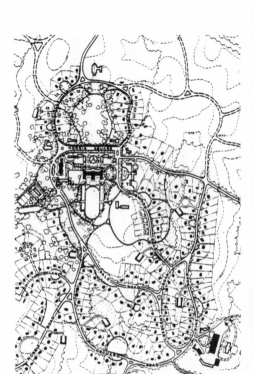

Norris, Tennessee. An unusual case in America, a suburban community thoughtfully and logically planned.

Housing in an intelligently planned community. Staff housing at the hospital in Paimio, Finland designed by Alvar Aalto, 1929–33.

146

A rare case of a major governmental building of thoughtful design; the Boston City Hall, a commission resulting from an architectural competition. Kallman and McKinnell (together with Edward Knowles in the competitive design submission).

Charles Eames's own home. A house made of industrial components of the kind used to construct modern factories. Interior of living space in the Eames house.

Although most furniture offered to the modern consumer is of notorious design absurdity, a variety of outstanding modern solutions to furniture problems exists, many of them the work of outstanding modern architects. This adjustable chaise was designed by Le Corbusier and Charlotte Perriand in 1928.

Modular storage furniture designed by Charles Eames.

China, silver (or stainless steel), glassware and other table equipment, like furniture, is most commonly of poor design quality. In the illustration, modern white Arabia china from Finland is at home with the modern vernacular of the French pitcher and glass coffeemaker and with the traditional Belgian painted sugar bowl.

Office furniture of interchangeable parts designed by Fritz Haller. It suggests a realistic view of the office as a workplace rather than as a ceremonial setting. The chair is by Charles Eames.

Electric typewriter from Italy designed by Ettore Sottsass.

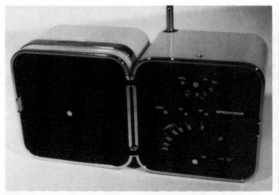

Brionvega portable radio from Italy designed by Marco Zanuso and Richard Sapper avoids such common absurdities as imitation wood-grain finish on plastic surfaces.

Contemporary textile design is often of high quality. A woven stripe designed by Alexander Girard.

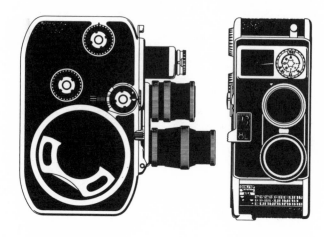

Cameras have a special ability to involve the interest and devotion of their owners-users. In most cases the best photographic equipment is also thoughtfully and expressively designed. Bolex moving-picture camera.

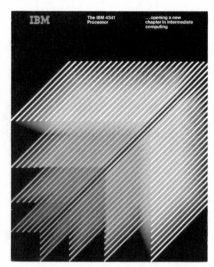

Graphic and advertising design of high quality is usually the work of an exceptional designer who has found support on the part of a client with a special design commitment.

Detail of a portion of a modern cargo ship.

Except for occasional ill-advised paint color schemes, aircraft are usually strikingly handsome. A Cessna small jet transport.

The most ubiquitous and influential of modern industrial products, the automobile, is most often an example of design chaos. This French Citroën strikes many observers as "odd" because it is logically designed and therefore unfamiliar in appearance.

Systems

THE MOST usual way of thinking about objects is to view each one as a separate, isolated unit unconnected with anything else. As human beings, we tend to see ourselves in this way. Each one of us is, we say, an individual, unique and separate from any other. A cat, a dog or a bird is a separate creature; an apple, an onion, a tree or a mountain are each given a name and thought of as units that can be counted up. Now, biological organisms are not as isolated as this way of thinking would suggest. Each person is dependent on supplies of air, food and water and must find ways to stay within a narrow range of temperatures in order to sustain life. Food supply may come from animals or plants, which turn out to have subtle interdependencies. Birds may eat insects, but insects pollinate plants. Plants must have sunlight, water and suitable nutrients. We are discussing, thus, a complex range of systems in which no element is truly independent of its connections into related systems.

When we turn to humanly made, inanimate objects, the idea of an independent, self-contained object seems more applicable. The process of manufacture—with its needs for materials, tools and power—may seem system connected, but a finished product can still appear to stand in isolation. A simple wood chair of the kind made for thousands of years, once created, is, in fact, quite an isolated, independent totality. It can last almost indefinitely, certainly through many human lifetimes, and it requires no fuel, power or other external connections to support its continued existence.

A large number of the simple artifacts of history have formed our habit of thinking of each thing as a unit to be planned alone without thought for its connections. A preindustrial house, for example, was such a fixed and isolated object. If one wanted water inside, it was carried in a bucket from a well. Waste disposal meant carrying wastes out and away. Heat and light came from separate objects (a stove, a lamp) which could be carried in and out without being in any way parts of the house. Observe, however, how many "improvements" begin to modify this splendid independence and isolation. A fireplace must be built-in and connected to a chimney. It is useless without a fuel supply, and without a chimney, will discharge smoke into the surrounding air. A flush toilet requires running water and a drain connection.

In characterizing modern life as focused on process rather than product, one is noting an increase in methods of doing things that involve systems of complex interconnections. Walking requires nothing but a walker. A horse-drawn vehicle is dependent on the availability of horses, which in turn need housing and feed, as well as suitable roads. A bicycle requires not only suitable roads and paths, but replacement tires and other parts. A railroad is typically called a railroad system, to denote a highly complex set of related parts. The locomotive requires fuel and water, lubricants and spare parts. It is useless without tracks, precisely matched to its requirements. Locomotive and track only exist to move the cars which must be matched to track, locomotive and one another. Switches, signals, stations, and all the other elements of the typical railway are tied into a total system that exists, not for the sake of objects that make it up, but for the process it makes possible.

Gradually, more and more everyday objects that make up our environment and establish the character of our lives are becoming like the railroad, a system. A telephone is only incidentally an object; its primary function is to give access to a system. A radio or television set is useless without access to power and without a system of broadcast programming for it to receive. An automobile needs gasoline, oil, water, tires, spare parts and roads on which to travel. A house is now only 25 to 50 percent structure; the balance is systemic equipment, electrical, plumbing, heating, air conditioning and appliances—all dependent on outside system connections, and all with a short life dedicated to process rather than to a lasting status.

The impact of these realities on the design of things has been extensive but, in many cases, only dimly understood and dealt with. We have all experienced the problems of a modern passenger airplane, capable of performing at an amazing level in its own independent function, but hopelessly bound by the failure of air traffic control, airport layouts and airline schedules so that its advantages are drastically reduced. Then, as passengers, we reach the airport and discover that it has no reasonable systemic connections to the community it serves. We inch for hours in traffic to travel the few miles from airport to town losing, in the process, all the time advantage that the airplane has gained us. In such a situation, we are victims of a typical modern problem, the system which has not been developed as a system. Aviation has no jurisdiction over the car, bus and road system to provide airport access. The location and building of airports is only dimly connected to flight functions, traffic patterns and city layout. Air traffic control is imposed after the fact to try to make some order out of a hopeless and dangerous jumble. It is powerless to relocate airports or make airline schedules rational. In such situations, we are facing a chaotic transitional stage, in which isolated objects have given way to limited systems, but the planning of systems, extended to a logical degree of comprehensiveness, has only been attempted in the most rudimentary way.

Military and naval systems, whatever one may think of their objectives, have been leaders in demonstrating the significance of extending interconnectedness to its logical limits. So many military failures of the past have demonstrated this point—men with guns but no ammunition, warships with guns, armour and ammunition but no fuel supply, or foiled by poor intelligence—that a systems approach has become characteristic of modern warfare. Space exploration projects, fed by systems of military origin, are the most advanced demonstrations of the advantages that accrue when objects are interpreted as links in a process rather than as fixed and lasting realities on their own account. A rocket, a space capsule or a planetary landing module is, in one sense an object, but it has none of the lasting stability of a castle, a cathedral or even a royal coach. These space objects are things made only to produce a result, to live a short life within a set of events, and then either vanish or, in a few cases, find their way as curiosities into a museum exhibit— souvenirs of the event, perhaps, but in no way objects of continuing usefulness.

This drift away from lasting and stable objects forming an environment of some permanence, that can be expected to change in only limited degree in the course of a human lifetime, has been going on for many years, but its full implications are only becoming visible as the drift accelerates. It seems now that every object makes demands for fuel, energy, air and ground space, and that it turns back to us a variety of problems relating to safety in use, to disposal of waste and, ultimately, to disposal of the object itself. The automobile is a prototypical example. Unlike a wheelbarrow, a sled or a cart, more like a horse but with exaggerated impact, it confronts us with its demands for costly and irreplaceable construction materials, a need for increasingly scarce operating fuel, land space for roads, and its extreme problems of safe operation and distressing output of wastes—gas as it operates, a massive carcass after it has become inoperative. It has been invented and designed in the light of a certain ideal vision, a vision of easy, independent mobility and fantastic attractiveness. The need to realize this vision has forced its development as, to some extent, a system component, but the full reach of its system connections has never been really thought about at all until the last few years, when the harmful consequences of its use have begun to catch up with, and overtake, its advantages.

The pattern that the automobile system demonstrates is destined to become more and more common. Our past has, in large measure, known only situations in which the impact of objects has been small and mostly beneficial. The wood chair discussed above used only a tiny bit of a plentiful material. It offered its owners considerable comfort over a period of generations at a tiny cost, with negligible problems in terms of safety, waste and other secondary consequences of its use. The total impact of the population's need for chairs created virtually no problems. Similarly, a primitive, or even a developed, house of preindustrial civilization, although it made larger demands for material and land space, constituted a net gain for its occupants and so for humanity as a whole. Its environmental impact, as we would now call it, was not seriously problematic and may even have been positive, since the superior shelter it provided probably reduced the need for fuel over its lifetime by far more than the amount of material needed for its construction.

Now a new house confronts us with a very different situation. Its first need, the requirement for land—apparently no problem when we consider the total surface of the earth—turns out to be a serious problem in the limited areas where great concentrations of human population have developed. Its energy needs have become vast and are supplied only by consumption of increasingly rare and irreplaceable fuels* and through a

---

*Atomic power, long promised as a solution to this problem, turns out to require a fuel in increasingly short supply (uranium) and cooling water even harder to make available—to say nothing of problems of safety and waste disposal.

net of services that is costly to build and maintain. It consumes water and generates wastes far beyond the minimal biological needs of its inhabitants. The materials needed for its construction are increasingly scarce and, in the case of aluminum, require enormous energy for their production. Although such a modern house may offer certain short-range advantages to its occupants, its demands are so great that it may easily show up as a net liability to humanity over its life span. Such issues will never be clarified as long as objects are developed and evaluated in isolation. The house itself, and many of its parts—window, bathtub, furnace or dishwasher—may be individually functional, well made and visually acceptable; yet in *system* terms, it may turn out to be disadvantageous to the total society and even to the individual user.

Such matters can go unnoticed for generations in a context where space and resources are vast in relation to the demands made on them. We are now deeply involved in a situation in which expanding demands are being made on resources that are becoming inadequate. As a result, we are being forced to examine every object in its relation to all the systems in which it participates. Functional evaluation cannot be limited to asking, "How well does it do its job?" We must add a long list of questions including:

1. What materials will manufacture consume?
2. What plant and equipment is involved in manufacture?
3. What are the waste by-products of manufacture?
4. What are the labor requirements of manufacture and the impact of this work on those who do it?
5. What will be the energy and material consumption demands resulting from use of this object?
6. What will be the space requirements and other environmental consequences of putting this object to use?
7. What possible or actual benefits and burdens will use bring to users?
8. What burdens (and benefits, if any) will use bring to nonusers?
9. Have impacts on health and safety of users and nonusers been considered in answering items 7 and 8 above?
10. What waste products will use generate and how will these be dealt with?
11. At the end of useful life, what problems will result from disposal of this object? Can the materials from which it is made be reused?

The reader can probably think of additional troublesome questions and will notice how each question in this list can be broken down into a number of subsidiary questions. The use of such a checklist will very quickly reveal that objects differ vastly in their level of isolation from systemic connections and in the degree to which they present problems to the society that builds and uses them. It may be interesting to compare the answers to the applicable listed questions to some selected pairs of objects. Compare, for example, an Indian tepee with a modern mobile home, or a violin with a snowmobile. We are in the habit of thinking that the *cost* of an object represents simply its purchase price, but it is becoming increasingly clear that this may be the least of its costs and that many of the real costs are, in the present state of affairs, not paid by owners or users but are shifted onto others in the present or future who may not reap whatever benefits the object in question has to offer.

Any such discussion of the systemic connections of objects must lead to a confrontation with one of the most universal systems in modern use, the system of using money as a means for bringing about exchange of costs and benefits. As much as most designers would prefer to avoid it, there can be no realistic discussion of design objectives without some consideration of the ways in which economics relates to the design of spaces and objects.

Economic Considerations

In a modern commercial society, not only are money issues involved in everything that occurs, they often appear to be determining factors. The systematic study of economics remains troublesome and puzzling to all but professional economists, who are themselves often unable to agree about even the most basic questions. It is not within the purposes of this book to attempt a clarification of these complexities, but it is appropriate to comment on the ways in which the design of the environment and its objects connects with the economic system, in order to avoid some common misunderstandings.

Efforts to design things as they should be, to create good environmental conditions—in the terms developed in previous chapters—often encounter problems and resistance in relation to the economic issue. As such problems surface, they are commonly described in some of the following ways:

1. Well-designed things and places cost too much and therefore cannot

be afforded or will not be accepted by the public—consumers or their political representatives.*

2. Since business is organized with an intention to maximize profit, it cannot or will not pay the extra costs to assure that design excellence characterizes its activities.

3. Since a large part of the consuming public prefers badly designed things, both public service and self-interest lead business to produce things that are badly designed.

4. Since business is competitive, the struggle for survival forces each business to do whatever will best meet or surpass its competition. This often means producing bad things for the reasons cited in item 3 above.

It is probably possible to list many similar and overlapping views that are constantly expressed in explanation or defense of the poor showing of the production of technological society. Examination of the four concepts will indicate the ways in which they express both partial truths and partial, misleading falsehoods.

It should be noted, first, that the concepts of costly, expensive and the opposite concepts of cheap or economical are used very loosely and in ways that can be confusing. There is a tendency to focus on first cost or price, money that must be paid now, as more significant than total long-range cost over the life of an object or a situation. Ordinary people are more subject to this mistake than businesses and other organizations, but those, too, tend to be influenced by feelings that a low price now is "a bird in the hand," while future benefits are uncertain and may only accrue too late to benefit those now involved. The average shopper will compare prices of new cars, washing machines or houses and will make some judgment about what can be afforded in absolute terms ("Can I find the money now?") and some judgment about the personal benefits that will derive from this expenditure, but it is a very rare shopper who makes any effort to consider *total* cost—including materials and energy consumed, cost of maintenance, cost of financing (or interest lost on cash invested), cost of space to be occupied, allowances for possible mishaps (accidents, for example), and cost of ultimate disposal. Before buying an automobile or a house, intelligent people will make some estimate of ability to meet at least the more obvious of these costs, but careful comparison between offered alternatives is surely very rare (and also very difficult). Businesses and other organizations often are

*Political representatives become involved when, for example, a school board selects a poor design in preference to a better one because it is cheaper.

more inclined to seek quality rather than low first cost because they habitually examine economic questions in the light of more sophisticated accounting techniques that probe real costs more fully. It is not coincidental that business machines, factory equipment and office and industrial buildings are usually made to higher design standards than the comparable consumer products. Another issue, related to the problem of discovering *true* and total costs, is the question of how to trace and evaluate costs that are, for various reasons, displaced and thus to some degree, concealed.

One of the primary objectives of a perfect economic system is to make any known goods or services available anywhere. The role of money is to make it possible for the beneficiary to compensate the true costs involved (including compensation to any intermediaries who have facilitated the transport and exchange required). In a perfect system, everyone would pay exactly what the benefits cost and would receive in exchange exactly matching benefits. In practice, such an equitable system is constantly subject to manipulation that has as its purpose displacement of costs and exaggeration of rewards. The concept of "buy cheap and sell dear" includes, in addition to the idea of reasonable reward for effort expended, the realization that shifting costs away from places where benefits accrue can be advantageous, however basically unfair. Economic man is constantly seeking means to shift costs away from himself and onto others to cheapen his benefits. Strategies to accomplish these ends are embodied in any number of situations and objects in the built environment. When a speculative builder buys farm land at a low price, subdivides it, builds houses on it and sells houses and land together at a maximum price (determined by market forces), he can expect to receive back all of the true costs of his investment in the land and construction, plus a profit that will reward his effort. In most cases, however, he will have managed to shift away from himself many of the costs of what he has done. The roads, water and sewer systems that the subdivision will require will be provided by the community. The buyers of the houses may discover, in due course, that they are faced with many costs for solutions to problems that the developer did not consider (drainage, landscaping, correction of defects in poor materials and workmanship, for example) as direct or indirect burdens in the form of increased taxes imposed by the community to cover the costs of extra police protection, road maintenance, schools and similar services ignored by the builder.

When the householder burns fuel in his furnace or in his car, he expects to pay for that fuel. He discharges the waste gases into the air, however, and, in so doing, shifts that portion of his fuel consumption costs away from himself and onto the whole community. Waste gases in the air attack the stone of city buildings, bringing about progressive destruction. The householders burning coal in stoves or gasoline in cars do not pay the costs of repair or replacement. Conversely, the person who buys something may find that the purchase price includes costs unrelated to any benefit he receives. The price of a package of cigarettes includes the cost of advertising the brand in an effort to improve its competitive position and to make cigarette smoking more attractive. It also includes taxes that will pay for various functions totally unrelated to his smoking that are imposed, in an often unrealized hope of discouraging the practice of smoking. Manipulations of the economic system to displace costs—whether undertaken for private gain or for the furtherance of public purposes—tends to make all discussions of true costs misleading. When continued over long periods of time, they also lead to distortions that bring about highly unfavorable results. Resistance to such distortions can come from market forces generated by a public able to recognize exploitation and resist it, or from governmental restrictions administered on behalf of the public in situations where the first, more direct route fails to operate. Most individuals would prefer that their automobiles be as safe as possible, but have failed to make this preference felt through market pressures. As a result, government restrictions have emerged as the only means through which the tremendous costs of unsafety in cars can be brought under control. This spreads the costs among all beneficiaries of automobile transportation, thus creating a significant motivation for design improvement.

Government regulation is itself subject to manipulation on behalf of special interest groups in an effort to bring about unfair shifting of costs. The decline and near collapse of the railroad system of the United States is a well-known example. Railroads maintained and paid taxes on their own trackage, stations and other facilities. But competitive systems of road and air transport successfully shifted many of their costs, such as the cost of road building and maintenance, of airports, air traffic and safety systems, onto the general public. As a result, in spite of its inherent high efficiency, railroad transportation gradually lost its economic advantages and expressed this problem in the imposition of direct, short-range charges for service. The competing systems, however, were able to offer seemingly lower charges for services that were in fact less economic. As a result, the cost of transportation for the total population has increased, for reasons that are not essentially economic ones, but express the successful manipulation of certain groups in shifting costs away from their proper and logical place.

Consideration of such issues may lead away from matters that directly concern design, but it is important to be clear that simple cheapness is not a reliable index of economic success. Nor is actual success or failure in economic terms a reliable index of design success in situations where arbitrary manipulation has distorted the direct working of logical economic principles. In fundamental economic terms, design excellence is destined to be economically sound almost by definition. Optimum functional performance with best use of materials and constructive techniques cannot be more costly than poor function and foolish or wasteful uses of materials and labor. In practice, this basic fact is constantly distorted and concealed by our limited and mistaken view of costs and by the successful manipulations of those who shift costs in such a way that, although they seem to have been avoided, they are simply being borne unjustly by those who do not benefit from the objects and processes involved.

If we now return to the list of four common protests that opened this section, it becomes possible to comment on each as follows:

1. Well-designed things do not cost too much if we view costs in their totality and if the costs in question have not been manipulated for the self-interest of particular individuals or groups in order to deliberately shift real costs into illogical places. Many well-designed objects are, in actuality, cheap by any standards, even first cost alone; conversely, an even larger number of excessively expensive things—in terms of first and true total costs—are disastrously badly designed. In case there may be any doubt about this matter, examples are offered.

2. Maximization of business profits involves a variety of complex strategies, among which determination of the design qualities of products plays only a small part. The idea that design excellence represents an extra cost, above a maximal profit level, is a fallacy. Quality in design is not the result of more costly processes, but rather of the simple intention to achieve excellence and the knowledge of how to achieve it. Many outstanding design achievements have come out of situations where there has been virtually no funding; many of our worst productions have been produced from generous budgets. Quality of design production has no reliable correlation with the funds expended.

3. Although there is ample evidence that the consumer public will often accept products of appallingly bad design, there is no clear evidence that these are actually preferred. They are rather accepted in the absence of reasonable alternatives and, most often, to the accompaniment of aggressive promotion through advertising. There is a parallel history of enthusiastic acceptance of well-designed products, even when these may be presented in ways that offer special difficulties. By careful selection of cases, it is always possible to offer evidence suggesting that well-designed products are destined to failure or very limited acceptance. A similar selection of cases can support the opposite viewpoint. In fact, market acceptance of products is largely controlled by other factors in which design is neutral, however unfortunate and absurd this circumstance may seem. From a strictly commerical point of view, a successful design or a design disaster stand an equal chance of succeeding in the marketplace. It might be otherwise if the consumer public were more aware of the possible positive impact of design quality. But, at least in the United States in the 1970s, it is impossible to claim that such a public exists on any large scale. There is not, however, any consistent evidence to support the opposite view: that whatever is worst will be most successful. Examples are offered here, again, in support of this contention.

4. Competition in business is concerned with such real issues as value offered in relation to price asked or cost-benefit ratio, as well as with certain more mythical issues concerning acceptance and loyalty based on irrational and artificially generated opinions of the consumer public. Design excellence can play a part in aiding competitive advantage in both the real and the mythical realms. The idea that a policy of deliberate production of inferior design will aid in either or both of these ways is the product of a curious kind of cynicism and contempt for the consumer public that infects some part of the business world. The belief that whatever is worse will sell best appeals to those who are inclined to produce whatever is worst. The erratic success of such a plan is matched by the equally erratic performance in the marketplace of products of a high level of excellence. In a pluralistic modern society, anything may have limited success or complete failure based on influences quite outside its own merits.

It should be noticed that the preceding discussion has been presented in terms that refer to the capitalistic, free enterprise systems of North America, parts of Western Europe and some Asian countries. In discussions of the comparative merits of this economic system versus socialis-

Many modest objects of obscure, traditional origin remain examples of design excellence along with economy. The simple French wine glasses made in a range of sizes are no less beautiful because they are inexpensive.

Among automobiles, the most economical turn out to be, again and again, the best designs in any other terms. The Model-T Ford, the Volkswagen and, in this illustration, the Austin Mini.

Bicycle history has involved a long evolution into the highly sophisticated types now available. Almost every bicycle is handsome and economical both in first cost and in performance.

The Thonet bentwood chair. Comfortable, sturdy, elegant in appearance and inexpensive.

tic and communistic systems, it is sometimes argued that one system or another favors the development of design excellence or creates some of the aberrations discussed above. On the basis of available evidence, such arguments appear spurious. In an effort to use design as a medium for propaganda or to please a large proletariat public, communist states have fallen into the very errors that occur in capitalist countries in the name of free enterprise. Socialist activities in the Scandinavian countries in the field of housing cooperatives, for example, have produced design excellence, but so has the coexisting private enterprise in these countries. Governments in all countries have an erratic record, sometimes sponsoring design excellence, sometimes not. The political inclinations of those involved seem to have nothing to do with the matter; it is rather a ·question of the knowledge and concern exercised by the decision makers who select professional designers and who approve or reject their work. Ironically, the governmental agencies least concerned with art and design—the military and naval forces—produce the highest levels of government-sponsored design in many countries.

One can deplore the declared need for an arms race while still observing that the products generated in its name are the result of a special kind of competition, more serious and more direct than the competition of trade. Economic pressures still operate in this area, however, primarily those of cost-benefit ratio. If we put aside our concern about the purpose of modern military weapons, we can consider the *way* they are developed as a prototype for study of the connections between design and economics.

The Luxo lamp, a brilliant solution to the problem of providing easy adjustability for position of light source with a minimum of structure and complexity. A most economical light source.

That connection is a matter of generating alternatives and then testing those alternatives against one another in terms of *real* benefits versus *real* and *complete* costs. The evolutionary process in nature is our textbook for study of this kind of competitive system and our laboratory demonstration as well. Although, in biological terms, what we do is part of the evolutionary system, the biological time scale is too slow to affect humanly generated technological and design evolution. If they are not artificially distorted or tampered with, and if their effects are not concealed, economic pressures serve the valid purpose of favoring whatever is truly best. It is our duty to seek out and evaluate these pressures, predict their effects and respond appropriately to them in our designs. Response to distorted, misdirected and misevaluated economic pressures can only lead to mistakes that are, in a genuine and deep sense, costly.

Special Concerns

The broad concept of satisfactory function implies that objects should do what is expected of them, but it also tacitly implies that they should not do other, objectionable things not expected of them. The whole focus of technological development, invention and creative design, for the last 150 years or so, has been concentrated on the positive side of this matter. We have designed things to *do* what we want done. In accomplishing our purposes, we have generated side effects, unwanted consequences of the main line of activity that are, in one way or another, objectionable.

The historical view of these side effects has been to ignore them on the grounds that they are a small price to pay for the advantages secured by the primary effort. This view has served well in a society with infinite space, resources and resiliency in relation to the activities it undertakes. When building cathedrals without any theoretical knowledge of engineering basics, it must be expected that there will be an occasional collapse. The harm done is completely outweighed by the achievements accomplished. It is reasonable to expect exploration of unknown oceans in tiny ships to result in a number of losses. Concentrating vast populations in towns and cities brings such great advantages in terms of easy communication, commerce and defense that the incidental problems of air quality, sewage disposal and disease seem a small price to pay.

The history of such developments has, until recently, been so successful in large terms as to have established a general point of view to the effect that progress will always turn out to be, on balance, advantageous and that its incidental problems can always be dealt with in some way as an afterthought. This attitude has dominated design activities over the ages. Le Nôtre, as he planned the fountains at Versailles, saw no reason to worry about what might happen to the waters of the Seine. The Wright Brothers were prepared to face whatever risks flight might entail, confident that they were nothing compared to what was being achieved. The discovery that DDT could wipe out objectionable insects was, at the time of its introduction, clearly a boon to humanity.

The same kinds of inventiveness could, after all, offer a vaccine to control smallpox, sewer systems to control the bubonic plague, fire companies to limit destructive fires and insurance to compensate any that suffered from uncontrolled hazards. Doubts that this kind of progress is always beneficial have surfaced very recently in the face of a growing population in a limited environment that can no longer absorb every distressing side effect with such ease, and in awareness of the magnitude of some side effects that challenge the advantages of the primary activity. Automotive transportation, for example, is everywhere perceived as tremendously advantageous in its primary role of providing easy, autonomous transportation anywhere at any time. Its side effects were for many years unnoticeable or negligible. But as the automobile accident becomes a primary cause of death, as air pollution threatens to make cities uninhabitable, as highways consume both land and financial resources to an extent totally disproportionate to their usefulness, and as irreplaceable natural resources are depleted, questions emerge as to whether specific kinds of technological convenience are humanly advantageous.

Such issues are now with us in every context, and it is no longer reasonable to undertake the design of anything at all without some exploration of the anticipated side effects. How can these be predicted, controlled and rendered at least harmless and, if possible, transmuted so as to be in some degree advantageous rather than destructive? We have not arrived at any clear point of view about ways in which to focus this kind of evaluation on what we do, but we have at least become aware of the importance of the issue. At present, we seem to have evolved a system in which such questions are dealt with through a kind of adversary confrontation. Those who want to do something (build a town, set up an atomic power plant, sell more and bigger automobiles, build more highways or dams) take a position asserting the advantages of these plans and making every effort to conceal or minimize any detrimental side effects. Recognition of hazards and troublesome consequences is left to a small, but increasingly vocal, protest group. These groups publicize the distressing possibilities of many modern technological advances and attempt to exert force to limit or control the inherent problems in the plans that are regarded as necessary aspects of progress.

Adversary confrontation in such matters has serious disadvantages, however. The parties in such confrontations are not inclined to make available to one another data to which they may have access, and a premium on distortion and concealment develops. Planning for action can only really be called responsible when it explores, voluntarily and without prejudices, all the possible consequences, even the most negative, and attempts to anticipate and deal with them.

Competent design, as it has been described here, must always include this kind of responsibility. That such responsibility is only erratically present among the design professions is one of the disgraces of modern times. No engineer would knowingly design a bridge in such a way as to make collapse a probability. But, under the pressures of commercial competitive practice, engineers design automobiles that are far less safe than the state of the art would permit. It has taken building codes, however inadequate and retrogressive, to force architects to make buildings even minimally safe against fire and collapse. Any number of products and packages introduce hazards and objectionable by-products into our life environment in ways that could, with some thought, be limited or controlled—often at no cost at all—if the inventors, designers and producers involved would show the necessary concern. In a general analysis of the nature of design, all these issues fall under the heading of function. Good function must be interpreted not only as doing what is intended, but also avoiding anything that might be objectionable. However obvious this might seem, it has become clear that everyone involved in creating the modern environment and its individual components must accept a new willingness to confront a checklist of concerns that are all too easy to neglect. As they have surfaced up to now, the primary headings are:

1. Environmental impact
2. Consumption of resources
3. Production of wastes
4. Safety
5. Impact on health

Each of these issues has been touched on earlier in this book, but each, when confronted as a specific concern, turns out to present unresolved problems in our thinking. In each case, we know of directions that can be labeled as favorable or unfavorable, but, in practice, we have no clear points of view to guide us in deciding what is reasonable. We like to anticipate the possibility of total success in regard to each or to all of these issues, but many of the projects we undertake make this difficult. It is hard to conceive of building a highway or a residential community with *no* environmental impact or a totally favorable one. A completely safe automobile, airplane or chain saw seems beyond hope. Many things we make may be problem free in one area, but not in another. A camera has little or no environmental impact, except that it does produce waste. A newspaper is not much of a safety or health problem, but it consumes resources and produces wastes. Chairs have little environmental impact, but their influence on health is greater, and more unfavorable, than is generally realized.

170

Each one of these issues can be explored in far greater depth than is appropriate in this book. From the point of view of design activities we need to remind ourselves that it is never reasonable to ignore totally any of these matters, nor to try to shift responsibility for them away from design. To merely meet legal requirements or public demands is hardly an adequate exercise of responsibility. But, what one can consider to be an adequate exercise of responsibility is, at the present time, less clear. There cannot be a sharp line of separation between satisfactory and unsatisfactory in relation to such issues. If there is clarity as to the directions that are desirable (safety is better than risk, less wastes are better than more), every project and every design proposal can at least be tested against each of these issues for optimum results within the knowledge and skills of the people involved. Any thought and effort turned toward improved safety in transport, reduction of wastes in packaging, control of environmental destruction in planning of highways is automatically an advance over the recently widely held view that all such issues are of such insignificance as to be almost totally ignored.

Another kind of newly developing insight that impinges on the conventional fields of design comes from the fields, still too new to have adopted a consistent name, sometimes called environmental psychology or studies in environmental behavior. It has long been recognized that the environment influences the ways people feel and, to some degree, the ways in which they behave. Planners, architects and designers have been aware of this for a long time in an informal way, but have been inconsistent in their concern and have not had access to any organized study of how this relationship works. It is commonly observed, for example, that some parks are much and well used, while others are misused or not used at all. While location and the nature of surrounding buildings may have some influence on the situation, it is also clear that the actual design of the park has a great deal to do with how people choose to use it. It has been suggested that poorly designed kitchens, in which two people will inevitably collide and irritate one another, may be a factor in developing family discords. The use of carpet in spaces that traditionally had hard surfaced flooring (such as school classrooms) tends to promote quiet and constructive behavior. The practice of filling subway stations and trains with cluttered and shoddy advertising materials may well be a factor in promoting littering and vandalism. Almost everyone has occasion to use spaces, buildings and objects so poorly suited to real needs as to stimulate some level of hostility toward whatever authorities can be identified as having created the situation.

All these points may seem obvious, but they have been constantly overlooked and, when they are recognized by designers, it is often difficult to get support for improvement in the absence of firm supporting data. The scientists, mostly psychologists and sociologists, who are interesting themselves in these matters are undertaking orderly research in an effort to correlate behavior with environmental circumstances and to develop usable and respected standards that can be used to make more situations supportive of constructive human behavior rather than hostile to it. Research is most effective at reporting on how situations have and have not worked out in the past, but techniques for projecting and advising on what might be best in future situations tend to lag behind to a degree that sometimes discourages working designers, who must make determinations about how things will be made and constructed, without waiting for lengthy tests in prototypes. Such tests are difficult to conduct, even when time and money are available, because of the difficulty of establishing truly controlled conditions that make results trustworthy in scientific terms. It is not of much use to know that a certain situation is problematic (crowded housing in a densely populated city, for example), unless the aspects that create problems can be identified and alternatives developed. It is the most intractable of problems that are most in need of this kind of study, but these are, in the nature of things, the problems that are least amenable to easy solutions.

The mere fact that a recognized field of study concerned with such problems has developed encourages us to hope that design can become more systematic in its relationship to human behavior. Success in this area is, in the end, its only reason for existing.

Design Method

In the considerable literature of art and design criticism, discussion is always concentrated on evaluation of results. The process through which results are achieved is dealt with, in the main, only in terms of technique. How paints are mixed and applied, how constructed perspective drawing is done, how clay or plaster are molded or stone carved, are all dealt with in various practical manuals. Comparable problems in architecture and design, the making of models, drawings and preparation of specifications are similarly covered. The creative as-

172

pects of painting or carving which result in a moving or even great work or in design to the evolution of a superior solution are rarely discussed. These elements of art and design are usually learned through study under a skilled master or through experience of repeated trials under criticism. In fact, there is often doubt about whether such creativity *can* be taught or learned. It is often said to be a matter of talent, presumably inborn and, although subject to development, a quality that cannot be generated if it is not present in the first place.

This view has led designers to trust talent, intuition and the skills developed through experience to lead them to good solutions to problems. The fact that this makes the design process something of a mystery has helped to promulgate the view that design skill is a rare and mysterious quality to be found only in a few, very extraordinary people. When designers are asked how they have arrived at an unusually successful, imaginative or exciting set of forms, they will usually report, quite truthfully, that they do not know. Phrases such as "the idea just came to me" are very common and it is tempting simply to concede that such creativity is not subject to rational explanation.

While this kind of view remains acceptable in the fine arts, modern design is so closely connected with scientific and technological fields, such as engineering and town planning, that we now need to explore more specifically the question of *how* design solutions can best be achieved. The need to teach design skills to ever larger numbers of people has encouraged this effort but, within the last few years, another and more pressing reason to explore the matter has surfaced. The techniques of computer data processing have demonstrated an ability to deal with, or at least aid in dealing with, a great variety of difficult and complex problems. The use of these techniques aids in solving engineering problems (design of aircraft structures, for example) on an everyday basis. The urge to apply these techniques to problems of architecture, town planning and other design activities has become very strong. In order to use computer techniques to deal with any problem, it is necessary to analyze and specify exactly, on a step-by-step basis, the *way* in which that problem is to be solved. Computers can be incredibly rapid and absolutely tireless in going through a vast number of steps in moving toward a problem's solution, but the steps must be specified and their logical relationships established before anything useful can be done.

Designers have thus been led to a new interest in exploring the mental processes that lead to good solutions to problems; what lies behind the special skills and intuitive methods that have been in use all through history? Although these are questions that are by no means fully answered, they have become a field for some serious study, usually under the designation "design methodology." If we accept the idea that design is a matter of arriving at solutions to problems, we are led into a study of the ways in which human thinking serves to further survival interests. It is surprising to discover that the nature of thinking has only occasionally been probed. We do not find it easy to describe how thought works. The following is an attempt to analyze thought in general and in the process of design.

1. The problem needing solution must be identified and stated with clarity. A problem not clearly identified or mis-stated can lead to aimless and disorganized effort which misses the point of the matter at hand. It is a common observation that a problem fully and clearly identified and stated is, as often as not, half-solved.

2. Information bearing on the problem and its potential solutions needs to be marshalled and made available in a clear and accessible way. The thinker, concerned with a particular problem, needs to have as much relevant information in memory as possible and, when the limits of memory are reached, overflow information at hand for consultation as needed. This aspect of problem solving is most often called research.

3. The step usually called creative can now be undertaken. Insofar as we understand the thought processes involved, they seem to consist of simultaneously holding the problem in mind while calling up from memory the specific information assembled through research and the more general information acquired through life experience, education and whatever other sources have stocked the memory with varied data. This information seems to be held in layers of memory that range downward from the recently acquired and easily accessible to the deep levels, usually called unconscious. The familiar effort of trying to think appears to be a deliberate churning of the resources of stored information held in the memory. As information comes to consciousness, it is matched against the perceived problem in an effort to find concepts, action proposals or forms that relate in some useful way to the problem at hand. When some piece of remembered information seems to connect with an aspect of the problem, we recognize a possible "fit"* in much the way the worker of a

*Christopher Alexander's *Notes on the Synthesis of Form* (Harvard University Press, 1964) explores the idea of "fit and mis-fit variables" as a key to problem solution.

jigsaw puzzle recognizes the shape of a piece as a possibility for a specific place in the incomplete puzzle. In this way, a potential solution, or part of a problem solution, surfaces and can be noted or stated as a proposal.

4. Each proposal for problem solution (usually only a fragment of the complete solution), once stated, is ready for testing in some concrete way—in words, drawings, models or prototypes that can then be evaluated in one way or another. At a simple level, the familiar sketch of an idea on a pad is such a test. It makes a proposed solution or part of a solution accessible to the imaginary testing that takes place as it is viewed and considered as it would work out if realized. Models and mock-ups permit more realistic testing. The tests of models in wind tunnels and test tanks, or of laboratory prototypes, are more literal tests of proposed problem solutions. Many such tests are necessary to lead thinking toward gradually better proposals. Each test leads to the next step, which is

5. Evaluation—aimed at sorting out what aspects of the proposal are successful and what aspects are not. This will usually make it possible to repeat steps 3 and 4 with a greater degree of success. This process of recycled proposal and evaluation can lead to gradually improving success, until a point is reached where the level of success is sufficiently good to suggest that further effort will not generate enough improvement to be worthwhile. The law of diminishing returns suggests that as an ideally perfect solution is approached, more and more effort offers less and less improvement. At some point it is appropriate to proceed to

6. Implementation (deployment) of the designed problem solution. When it is realized and put into use, certain shortcomings will usually be discovered that confirm the theoretical tests of step 4. As time passes, the original problem statement may become obsolete and new information will become available—until, after the passage of some time, the entire process can be undertaken afresh from the beginning. We say "the problem has changed" and therefore the old solutions have become inadequate.

It is in this process that the computer can be put to work to help in problem solution. Relevant data must be fed into the computer memory in usable form, the logical requirements of the problem must be established and programmed. The creative step can then be converted to an endless number of trial solutions in which a proposal is generated at random and tested for success as the significant data are processed in relation to the proposal in the light of the logic which is part of the problem statement. An evaluation is generated which can then be compared with a next randomly generated proposal. Very quickly, better and better proposals can be developed by retaining and developing whatever is evaluated as better and rejecting whatever is worse.

Factory layout is an example of the type of design problem that can be worked on very effectively in this way by computer techniques. The pieces of equipment and machinery, the materials to be stocked, and similar realities of the given problem are relatively easy to state. The requirements of an ideal solution in terms of efficient process flow are also easy to state. By attempting innumerable successive layouts and evaluating each against the given standards, progressively better layouts can be readily and rapidly derived. A human planner, using his brain in the same way, may do as well or better, but may also do less well, since habits and prejudices may inhibit the development of certain proposals and the time involved in each proposal will retard the number of trials and evaluations that can be attempted.

Computer aid has been most helpful in problems that have only one or very few criteria for success, but a large number of elements that must interrelate in a complex way to bring about that success. As the criteria for success become more numerous and their interrelationships become more complex, human thought seems to gain on the computer. The analysis that has gone into preparing problems for computer solution (or attempted solution) has gone a long way toward making the process of creative design more understandable. It has also helped to remove the process from the shadow of irrationality that has hung over it in the past.

Systematic thinking about design method has also helped to clarify another matter involved in every design problem: the resolution of conflicts. We want an object to be durable, but inexpensive. We want a room to face south to receive sun, but north for an attractive view. A typewriter should be light for portability, but heavy for sturdiness and immobility while in use. The most important parts of the designer's work concern his decisions to favor one side or another of such conflicts, or to arrive at compromises that balance the conflicting pulls equitably. The idea of the resolution of forces in physics has been known and used in many practical contexts for a long time. The navigator, who must consider wind, currents and the speed and course of his vessel in plotting his course and time of arrival, makes use of vectors in a parallelogram of forces to find out what he needs to know. A vector is a graphic (or mathematical) representation of a force having a direction and magnitude. It is usually diagrammed as an arrow with a length scaled to magnitude and a direction matching the direction of the real force. A northeast wind at ten miles per hour might be diagrammed thus:

A ship steering a course due west at 20 miles per hour exerts a force diagrammable:

Where the ship will actually go and how fast it will move can be discovered by "resolving" these forces in this diagram:

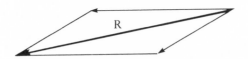

The resultant R tells us the direction in which the ship will actually move and, by measuring R, we can discover that its speed will be 27.9 miles per hour. The clarity and precision of the force parallelogram results from the ease with which the magnitude and direction of the forces can be stated. The forces that design must resolve do not usually have such clarity, but the concept is still useful, by analogy, in suggesting ways in which the varied pulls of conflicting purposes can be visualized, diagrammed and brought to resolution.

In regional planning and highway engineering, the selection of a routing for a new highway has always posed very difficult problems. Many conflicting forces—the value of land, the presence of communities and buildings, the geological realities that make construction difficult or easy, and many other pressures—all interact to make good judgments about the location of the highway very difficult, perhaps beyond the capacity of ordinary commonsense thinking. A technique has been developed in which a series of maps are prepared for the stretch in question, each one showing the ease or difficulty characterizing every part of the area in relation to a particular value.* In practice, this means that

*This technique is summarized by Christopher Alexander in his contribution to Gyorgy Kepes' *The Man-Made Object* (George Braziller, 1966), and is discussed more fully in Ian McHarg's *Design with Nature* (Doubleday, 1971).

*Ian McHarg maps charting Staten Island
as to residential suitability,*   unsuitability *for urbanization*

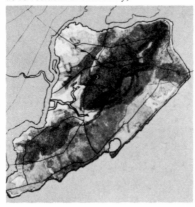

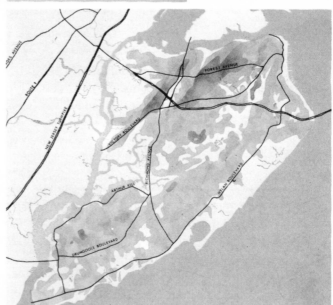

and, through superimposition, suitability *for urbanization.*

each map is covered with a graph paper square grid and each square is then marked with a grey tone on a scale from black to white, with the grey tone indicating the degree of difficulty that particular square represents for highway construction. Cost of land acquisition, difficulty of engineering construction, presence of obstacles (physical or otherwise) are thus all symbolized in a way that has a common denominator. The maps are then superimposed and, by projection or print through, made into a single map in which the grey tone density signifies difficulty of routing. The best route is simply the band of lightest tone between the points to be connected. The relative importance of the various considerations can be symbolized by adjusting the density of the tone of the various maps to explore alternative routes which would favor cost of construction, environmental issues or any other pressures at any level of relative importance. The same process can be conducted with even more precision by computer techniques, in which numerical values are given in place of grey tones for each issue and each map square.

Whether or not the specific technique is useful in relation to any particular design problem is less important than the insight that the technique gives into the nature of the thought processes involved in all design situations where varied positive and negative pressures must be resolved in relation to a physical, finite setting.

The hazards in using any such techniques arise from the limitation that confines them to dealing only with the specific considerations fed into them as inputs. They relate these values in accordance with whatever specific quantified values they have been given, and they generate very specific results that do not, in themselves, disclose the underlying generative considerations. It is easy to believe that a proposed plan generated by such sophisticated technique is inevitably and unchallengeably right and overlook the fact that it is no more than a necessary and accurate result of the information and judgments used to derive it. Direct human judgment may be more prone to error, prejudice, ignorance and stupidity than a computer, but it can handle a larger number of variables in a more subtle way and is more accessible to question and challenge. Organized method seems at its best as a guide, a stimulus and a corrective to unaided thinking. At least at the present time, mechanized method has not succeeded in offering serious competition to conventional methods of design, but it has encouraged a new clarity of thinking about what that conventional method is. To that extent, it has probably brought about a new and more rigorous design standard.

The Future
9

THE STRUGGLE to find a way to create an environment suitable to modern times has been going on for more than a hundred years, and is by no means complete. The group of historical events that have brought about a discontinuity in the developmental progress of design history is usually called the industrial revolution or, more colloquially, the coming of the machine age. It is customary to date this transition at about the middle of the nineteenth century. Since some hundred and twenty years have passed since then, it is easy to feel discouraged that ideas with us for so long a period have not yet brought about a new utopia or, at least, a society and environment as stable and logical as those of the Middle Ages in Europe or ancient Egypt. In our impatience, we are inclined to say that the machine age has come and gone, or that we are at least passing into a new phase of that era.

Lewis Mumford, in *Technics and Civilization* (Harcourt Brace, 1934) has suggested that we are at the end of the "paleotechnic" or early machine age and are passing into the "neotechnic" or *new* machine age. He characterizes these periods in a very perceptive way. The first phase is typified by the true machine—an assembly of parts based on an analysis of the work to be done in a way that parallels the rationalization of labor in the industrialized factory, where tasks are broken into parts, which can then be efficiently mechanized. The characteristic machine replacing human, animal or water power is the steam engine with its ingenious mechanisms, all based on the laws of physics which had been discovered and stated only shortly before they found application in this kind of mechanization. Mumford's neotechnic era, emerging as he wrote in 1934, involves a move away from the early machine of pistons, levers and governors. The new machine is more likely to be a turbine, converting energy into rotation more directly and more efficiently. The easy transfer of power in the form of electricity makes the electric motor a characteristic machine, portable and easily dispersed far from the actual point of generation of power. Communication by rail or ship is more and more replaced by telegraph, telephone, radio and television. Although they were in 1934 only hinted at, jet aircraft, spacecraft, factory automation, electronic data processing and nuclear power are all clearly characteristic elements of the neotechnic period, that might be dated at about mid-twentieth century.

Reyner Banham's title, *Theory and Design in the First Machine Age* (Praeger, 1960), clearly implies a similar conception, although Banham does not state it quite so specifically. He is rather concerned with the first wave of modernism in design as an effort to express a "first machine age," which roughly matches Mumford's paleotechnic period. We are led to conclude that, as we leave this age behind, we can expect that expression to become increasingly obsolete. Both of these writers have succeeded in stating a conceptual framework that helps to create understandable order out of events that are developing at what seems to be a constantly accelerating pace, making it impossible to assimilate one development before it is made obsolete by a successor. Alarm over this situation is a widespread modern reaction, and the literature of "futurism," for example Alvin Toffler's *Future Shock* (Random House, 1970), spells out the very real reasons for deep concern over whether humanity can adapt to the changes and the rates of change that are becoming current.

It seems possible that Banham and even Mumford are understating the magnitude of the changes involved in the technological revolution and are, in some, quite unintentional way, misleading us when they describe successive "ages" spaced about one hundred years apart in terms that suggest periods roughly comparable to well-recognized periods of earlier history—the early Renaissance followed by the high Renaissance, for example. We stand so close to the developments of the technological revolution, actually surrounded by their on-going progression, that it is very difficult for us to make accurate judgments as to what events are pivotal and what are incidental. We are thus in constant danger of accepting as sound, conceptual statements about our own times that actually distort real events.

The primary source of distortion in our understanding of contemporary events has to do with a time-perspective distortion that tends to make recent times important to us, while more distant events fade from our awareness. We feel that the last few hundred years of history have been crowded with important developments, and that the most important events of all are those happening within our own lifetimes. Paradoxically, this distortion can lead us to underestimate the importance of events in our own times as we try to correct our judgments by comparing recent events with past ones. It is suggested here that recent technological developments are being currently understood in ways that embody *both* of these errors.

The idea that the coming of the machine age was a development comparable to the coming of the Middle Ages or of the Renaissance *underestimates* the magnitude and impact of this development. The idea that we have passed through that revolution and that a new period is developing *over*estimates the significance of the changes identified by Mumford with the change from "paleo" to "neo" phases. The identification and naming of historical periods leads us into an assumption that the increment of change from each period to the next is approximately equal. Faced with change on a scale of magnitude never before experienced within recorded history, it is easy to miss the scale of that change and prematurely announce its completion.

Comprehension of the scale of time duration, once the periods in question go beyond a human generation or two, becomes very difficult. Very large figures tend to become meaningless—a billion does not seem very different from a million to any ordinary understanding. A useful exercise is to convert numerical statement of time periods into graphic equivalents, which can be seen in some more tangible way. For example, a table of time durations can be drawn up as follows:

Industrial revolution to the present	=	130 years
Renaissance to present	=	550
Fall of Rome to present	=	1,300
Recorded history	=	4,000
Human life	=	1,700,000
Any life on earth	=	3,500,000,000
Existence of earth	=	4,700,000,000

Suppose that this is converted to graphic form at a scale of one inch equals 1,000 years. The industrial revolution will represent one-eighth inch and all of recorded history will stretch for about four inches. Thus:

Fall of Rome   1850

2000 BC   0   1976

The span of human life will extend for about 11 or 12 feet, all life for about 60 *miles* and the life of the earth for about 80 miles. If we change scale so as to make the period of all human life fit on a book page, all of recorded history will become so small that it can be only viewed through a microscope.* When thinking about history in this scale context, the periods that can be identified with a spacing of a century or two begin to seem too small and trivial to be significant. Since the beginnings of humanity, we can identify only one truly basic change, so drastic as to have altered the quality of human life. This was the change, thought to have occurred between 8,000 and 10,000 years ago, that introduced agriculture and the domestication of animals, so that fixed settlements could replace a strictly nomadic life. This is the change that is usually called "the beginning of civilization" and it has still not encompassed all of humanity. With our larger time perspective, it may seem remarkable that a comparable change in human life can now be taking place, so soon after this first great change—and yet that appears to be the case. If that first change, the introduction of civilization, is not yet complete after more than 8,000 years, it should not be surprising that the change now in progress should be incomplete after less than 500 years. "Less than 500 years" is a hint that this change should be viewed as more extensive than the changes of the industrial revolution that date back only about 150 years and that can be considered largely accomplished.

The change that we are experiencing is actually on a much larger scale and may well take a thousand years or more to accomplish, if indeed it is ever successfully accomplished. The history of human civilization has been a history of developing technology. Unlike any other species, human beings invent solutions to problems and embody inventions in artifacts that aid human life, improve its quality and increase survival possibilities.

There is, however, one key human invention that is not totally materialistic. It is language, a system for the communication of ideas that may relate to objects, but also may not. If we can somewhat generalize our concept of language so that we do not restrict the term to the language of words, but include all the proto-linguistic systems of communication, such as mathematics, music and art, we are describing an invention oriented toward form in the abstract sense. This invention of conceptualization, or abstract thought, is too old to have any known

*To be exact, if the span of human life is scaled to 4 inches, all of recorded history will measure about 1/100 inch, a century 1/4000 inch.

184

date of origin, but it appears to be uniquely human and to be a special tool of whatever success the human species has achieved.

We are accustomed to a view of life that separates reality, in the sense of physical objects and circumstances, from ideas, thought or conceptualization, by which we mean the abstractions which we can internalize as form as distinct from chaos. Reality is full of form and, as we make or alter our reality, we give it new form. In the end, the form is what we know and understand, not the reality of random and incomprehensible material. Philosophy and religion have struggled with the apparent conflict between form and substance, idea and object, and have developed a view of a two-level reality, the twin realities of the concrete and the abstract, the material and the conceptual.

The revolution that we are experiencing is not at any such trivial level as a technical or political revolution. It is rather a discovery that this age-less dichotomy is no longer valid; that physical, material reality and the realities of abstract thought, of form, are interchangeable and are in the process of fusion. Human life, for the last 500 years, has been bound by a belief in a material reality of mass, substance and solidity; and human efforts at altering and improving this reality have been concentrated on manipulation of solid, material substance. Communication, language, has been only an incidental tool to aid in this manipulation.

The invention of language with its impact on thought was a first step away from the old reality of material objects and into another reality of concept and form. Because of a dominating concern with the reality of solid, physical material, it has been customary to view the realities of language and of art as incidental, secondary adjuncts to the true reality. The environmental circumstances, the designed objects of history, are all conceived in terms of this older solid reality. The pyramids of ancient Egypt are nothing if not solid, massive and material. That they are also works of art and have power to move us, results from the way in which they are formed, their geometric shape and positioning; but these aspects of their reality seem to us still in some way incidental, merely conceptual, and in no way as important as the simple physical mass of their structure. The building of buildings and towns, the making of all sorts of objects, has always been seen as a technique for manipulating physical materials in a way that will confer physical advantages. Roofs keep out weather and wheels make it possible to roll. Human needs for invented aids to survival have been so demanding as to make a concentration on materialistic technology an inevitable first priority.

As far back in history as we have any information, there have been hints of an emerging realization that the concepts with which language deals may equal, control and dominate the realities of physical mass. To seek shelter in a cave is to use the physical mass of the earth as a natural device to give advantages to human life. To pile up stones or create a cave of snow exploits mass for life improvement. The discovery that greater advantage can still come from introducing heating into the artificial cave involves an invention in which mass is secondary. The key to its effectiveness is a use of energy that will reduce the need for mass. A tent of skins on poles, heated by a fire, is superior to a stone hut with thick walls and uses only a tiny fraction of the mass of material.

The technological revolution that has occupied recent history is concerned with a change in emphasis from concentration on material and mass to a concentration on energy and its uses. Gunpowder is an invention for producing a sudden and violent release of energy. It quickly made the castle and the town wall obsolete. Picking up natural philosophy where the ancient philosophers had left off, the Renaissance began the investigation that we now call science and began to find the way to more and more inventions which, like gunpowder, used energy to achieve previously impossible results, or that reduced dependence on massive material. The industrial revolution put the discoveries of science to work in inventions, primarily mechanical inventions, which reduced or eliminated the need for human labor as a power source, making possible all sorts of activities and processes that depend on the management of vast quantities of energy. The impact of this revolution has been to move human attention away from objects and toward process and performance. The statement that modern, technological society is more materialistic than any previous society is only true if we regard preoccupation with energy and process as a form of materialism. Previous societies were more seriously concerned with objects than we are today. A medieval house was intended to last for generations and was expected to be the cornerstone of its owners' life environment. A modern house is usually only occupied for part of a generation by any one family—many tenants may use it during its life, and that life is likely to be short, possibly only fifty years or so. The occupants of this modern house do not depend on its solid mass for their comfort as much as on its mechanical systems, its heating, plumbing and lighting and its equipment—all devices for converting energy to some sort of advantage or comfort. The cost of the mechanical equipment exceeds the cost of the structure, and the energy consumed in the course of the house's life can easily represent two or three times the cost of the house

186

itself. Le Corbusier's statement that "a house is a machine for living in" is thus not merely a statement of an intention; it is a description of the literal fact of modern life and applies to every house, whether its appearance can be called modern or not. The house is simply a device in which energy can be converted to usefulness.

It seems to us now that the development of the industrial revolution occurred quite rapidly within an easily identified few decades. The shift from an emphasis on mass to an emphasis on energy is not nearly so specific an event. Energy was a factor in preindustrial civilization, and its use in industrialization is always through the medium of solid, massive objects. Objects are still very much with us and will continue with our civilization into the indefinite future. We are not giving up objects in exchange for process; we are simply shifting our interest from an era where the ratio might have been 80 to 20, to an era where the ratio is closer to 20 to 80. The change is not one that is already complete; it is a change too large and too basic to be accomplished in a mere hundred years or so. Rather, it is a change—still in progress—with beginnings in the Renaissance and a conclusion still somewhere ahead—possibly centuries ahead.

The shift from the paleotechnic civilization to the neotechnic that Mumford described is, in this view, an intensifying step within the larger transition from the realities of the past to the realities of the present. It is not a movement into a truly different human environment, but a step from a first to a second level. An example may make the point more clear. Throughout earlier history, sea transport depended on vessels powered by oar or wind. In either case, the boat as an object was the key invention; its way of using energy was primitive and so unreliable as to make sea travel only marginally practical. The industrial revolution supplied the ship with steam power with rapidly increasing success. The ship became more massive, but its mass was a device for making energy effective in delivering the desired performance. An ocean liner deployed a massive tonnage of steel in order to give its engines a vehicle for performance. This describes a paleotechnic solution to a problem of transport. The neotechnic solution is, on the face of it, an improbable one. Human beings have had dreams of flying over the ages, but those dreams have been concentrated on the vision of an experience of adventure and freedom. In realization, flight has been made possible by more successful energy management and has demanded a minimization of mass (weight). The modern transport airplane is of small mass, but expends a vast intensity of energy to achieve its effectiveness. The

The Cunard liner Mauretania *of 1907.*

ocean liner *Mauretania* of 1907 had a mass (weight) of 44,600 *tons* and carried, when new, 2,335 passengers. A Boeing 707 jet aircraft weighs about 115,000 *pounds* and can carry 179 passengers. The *Mauretania* could maintain a speed of 25 knots; the Boeing 707, about 600 knots. In an hour the ship could deliver 58,375 passenger miles; the aircraft can deliver 107,400 passenger miles, although its mass is only about 1/800 that of the ship.* In terms of energy expended, the 50,000 pound thrust of the aircraft's jets at speed and at altitude is almost exactly equal to the 70,000 h.p. of the ship's engines. Approximately the same amount of power is thus delivering about twice the performance when put to work in a device of 1/800 the weight. As seen by the user (passenger), the advantage is even more striking, as a journey that took five days is reduced to seven hours or less, a reduction in time expended of about 1:15. Any number of similar examples can be discovered, in which the modern ability to make use of massive amounts of energy has made possible the elimination or reduction of weight and has produced spectacularly improved performance, often with a reduction in energy requirements for a given unit of performance.

Our present situation may well represent the peak of the technological changeover from the use of mass to the use of energy as the primary technique for the expansion of human life advantage. The problem areas of contemporary technology, the problems of resource depletion, of pollution and waste disposal and of safety all are associated with the current massive emphasis on energy consumption. The early technologies of material and mass introduced a few problems in these areas, but they were minor compared to those that are now endemic. Objects use material and show up as scrap after they have outrun their usefulness and some can create hazards, but energy consumption on a scale that dominates life to the extent now current multiplies these problems by an enormous factor. The combination of dependence on energy with an accelerating increase in population now threatens to exhaust the reserves of fossil fuels within a very small number of years, and hopes for solving this problem through the use of nuclear fuels are now diminishing as the associated problems are more realistically recognized. Learning to make full use of natural energy sources (solar, geothermal, wind) and biologically renewable fuels (wood) is a useful

*To be exact, the ship weighed 44,640 tons or 89,280,000 pounds, the airplane 114,800 pounds; a ratio of 780:1. In terms of passenger miles delivered per hour, for each pound of weight, the ship produced .000065, the jet .93—about 14,000 times the result per pound!

direction, but it can only be effective if combined with a retreat from the massive energy consumption that has developed as the prime characteristic of the neotechnic era, the second machine age.

It may seem difficult to find any basis for optimism in this direction, but there are discoverable hints that we are in the process of entering a new phase of development that will shift away from the current emphasis on energy consumption as the only solution to almost every problem. This shift is not a response to the pressures of coming shortages; it is an acceleration in a line of development that has been under way for a long time—possibly through all of human history. It is the line of inventive thought that is less concerned with material mass and with energy consumption, and more concerned with the organization of information—that is to say, with form. Using material as a prime means of improving a life situation must always involve some expenditure of energy and the process must be directed by some conceptual or formal intentions. Nevertheless, the old view of things was mostly concerned with material. The effectiveness of the walls of a city or castle is primarily because of their mass. Once built, energy is no longer a concern, and their exact form was, in earlier times, almost accidental. The industrial revolution, with its new skills in using energy, did not dispense with solid mass; it used less to obtain the same result or managed to accomplish greater results with the same materials. In the process, concern with form and concept increased. Defense of a city with artillery means reliance on energy. The guns themselves are still massive, and walls and fortifications could still be effective to some degree if properly shaped.

The step which we are now in the process of taking will not eliminate concern with material and energy, but it will bring both of those aspects of reality under new controls, more precise and more sophisticated than we have known previously. Just as the shift from rail and ship transport to aircraft meant a reduction in use of mass and an increase in use of energy, so a shift to space travel means a new dependence on the precision of direction and control. The orbiting spacecraft is a small energy user and its mass is reduced to a minimum. Its effectiveness comes from the remarkable systems for precise communication and control. Ancient and medieval industry worked with solid materials, using human strength, with a little help from animal and water power, to make things from available materials. The factory of the industrial revolution substituted the power-driven machine for human effort. The factory worker is typically a machine operator and the smoke from factory chimneys is an indication of the energy conversion involved in running the machines. While the mill of the nineteenth century and the assembly line plant of the early twentieth century are still characteristic of modern industry, a new kind of industry is emerging.

The automated factory uses computer controls in place of machine operators to govern the way energy generates process. The products of modern factories are often less mass-material oriented than were their earlier prototypes. A radio of 1930 was a large wooden credenza-like case, containing many pounds of metal chassis, heavy transformers, large glass vacuum tubes and similar hardware. A radio of the 1970s is likely to use transistors and printed circuits of tiny size, assembled with minimal human participation into a small case, whose size is determined more by the need for dials and speaker than by its inner working components. It may well be tiny and weigh only a few ounces, but its energy needs can be fed from miniature batteries instead of involving hundreds of watts of line power. Both the product itself and the plant that produces it are dominated by the information management that we call their engineering. There is material present and energy to make it perform, but these have been reduced to a point approaching the threshold of human perception. A complete radio (except for its knobs and speaker) can be printed on a tiny chip. Small battery electrical energy is well below the human ability to experience it as shock. The physical realities of such a radio have almost disappeared; what remains is conceptual organization that makes it operative and the resultant performance.

A comparable sequence of development can be traced in many contexts where the terms mass and energy may not be strictly applicable but where a parallel transition is taking place from past methods of management to futuristic management techniques focused on information. Consider, for example, the problem of exchange of goods and services. In ancient and primitive societies, the barter of goods was routine. Wealth meant cattle, grain, land or some other real substance. The invention of coined money is a step toward a symbolic form of barter, which still, however, uses metals of value for the coins, combining symbolic worth with the value of a real metal which can be melted down and bartered. The emphasis on paper money and the check developed with the industrial revolution. The idea of credit is, in its way, comparable to the substitution of energy for material, in a focus on process rather than objects. Wealth becomes more and more a matter of ownership of securities—mere papers that stand for realities of process as much as for realities of property. The transition is moving onward toward a situation in which paper, as a symbol of value, can be replaced by invisible information stored magnetically and managed electronically. We already accept payment of taxes by withholding, payment for goods by presentation of a coded card which communicates directly with a data processing station. One can buy or sell securities with a phone call and most investors no longer take delivery of actual paper securities. The so-called "checkless society" is becoming a reality. In it, money will only be useful for trivial transactions. Income will be credited electronically and payments made (in many cases automatically) in the same way. The financial situation of any individual or organization becomes, in these terms, strictly a matter of information which has need neither for real goods or symbolic money in continuing the management of economic affairs.

It is possible to trace a comparable sequence of change in any number of fields; not necessarily with exactly synchronized steps, but with a rough time correspondence. When viewed in this way, all of the developments of the Renaissance, the eighteenth century, the industrial revolution and the accelerating changes of the present appear as *one* unified change—a change comparable to the change from the primitive world of the nomadic, hunting societies to the civilization of agriculture and cities. In relation to this time scale, distinctions between paleotechnic and neotechnic, between first machine age and its present successor, become small intermediate steps, bunched close together in time, in a major change which, because of its vast magnitude, requires centuries to complete. An attempt to diagram this change in relation to a time base might lead to the following chart:

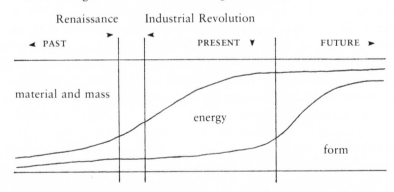

This suggests that all of civilization, from its beginning through the Middle Ages, was relatively unchanging in most basic ways. The materials available for human constructions remained the same (wood, various types of masonry and some minimal metals for special purposes)

and the extent of human knowledge also remained fairly static. At the end of the Middle Ages, little more knowledge was available to humanity than had been available in ancient Greece—in many fields actually less was available. It also suggests that, as the present period of transition is worked through, a future of some similar stability might be projected. It is obvious that projection of the current rate of change in most things (population growth, energy use, resource consumption) leads to predictions of imminent major disaster. The pessimistic view that this will be the course of events may prove to be correct. The alternative, a transition into an era in which knowledge, the management of information and a reliance on form become dominant is an equal possibility. Material and energy may be expected to retain their inevitable roles as the physical basis of reality, but their past and present dominance as the key aspects of reality will be diminished by the new reliance on form and pattern. An indication of what this can mean is already clear in the awareness of modern physics that mass and energy are interchangeable aspects of the same realities. Nuclear physics is, in the end, less concerned with either mass or energy than with the conceptual patterns that are the keys to both aspects of the real world.

The ancient and continuing desire to see the future always implies that the future is, in some way, an existing, predetermined reality which, if we could only "know" it, could be met in some advantageous way. That the nature of the future is to a major degree a matter of our own choosing, limited only by the basic relationships of cause and effect, and by the constraints of physical reality is, in many ways, so awesome a prospect as to frighten us back into a superstitious belief in a predestined course of events. And yet, we are surrounded by evidence that past choices of certain courses of action have inexorably shaped future environments and events.

Choosing to cling to the reliance of the past on solid, massive, material reality as the primary tool for human advantage, or choosing to press forward with constantly expanding uses of energy for the same ends, appear both to be choices that can only lead to an increasingly rapid build-up of disastrous problems, bringing about the end of human life (and perhaps all life) in the near future. We can already discover innumerable developments that suggest a growing dependence on the control of form, pattern and information and understanding of the power of abstract concept. It is not as clear that we have yet faced the need to diminish our dependence on material and, more recently, on energy. We still tend to think that *growth* is inevitable and desirable and seek a constantly increasing gross national product. "No growth" is only now being mentioned, rather cautiously and in limited contexts, as a possible future goal. The goal of contraction and shrinkage, in all matters of materials, things, and processes, is still hardly a possibility that anyone dares to mention. The concept of progress expressed as growth in ideas, information and in the quality of processes, seems still too new to have attracted vocal partisans. Nevertheless, if we choose it, this is the direction that appears to have the greatest potential for solving the problems that burden present-day life, and of evolving a stabilized future in which life's traditional physical burdens will be minimized, and the great potential opened up by the scientific and industrial revolutions will be realized.

In such a future, the basic human needs for food, shelter, health care and similar necessities could be provided with minimal consumption of materials, with energy supplied from permanently available sources (solar, geothermal, biologically replaceable fuels) and through the use of highly efficient techniques of production that place small reliance on human work. As Buckminster Fuller has pointed out in many of his talks and writings, modern technology makes it possible to provide for all of human basic needs with a per capita work load of only a few hours, perhaps eventually only a few minutes, per day.* As this long dreamed of, utopian possibility begins to become a reality in this century, our failure to understand it and to manage the resulting economic and political changes has turned it into a threat of widespread unemployment, accompanied by a burdensome leisure, likely to be used in wasteful or destructive ways.

The commercial world and the political forces that it influences tend toward false solutions in which employment of a boring and depressing kind can only be provided by producing a vast variety of almost useless products that can then be "consumed" via the expenditure of wages earned in this dull process of production. In developed countries we have, as a result, populations that must still work full time at dull, assembly line production jobs in order to afford subsistence plus saturation with costly products of questionable usefulness. The individual can expect to work hard (perhaps building unneeded highways, or in a factory manufacturing snowmobiles) in order to afford to buy cigarettes that are dangerous to health, a second car or television set, air conditioning for a dwelling that is improperly planned and sited, and to pay

*Utopia or Oblivion (Bantam Books, 1969).

Crown Hall, the design and architectural school building on the campus of Illinois Institute of Technology by Mies van der Rohe.

The Buckminster Fuller dome housing the U.S. exhibit at Expo '67 in Montreal.

for the energy, fuel, maintenance and health costs that all of these things create.

Buckminster Fuller's statement that our goal should be "to do more with less" and Mies van der Rohe's more cryptic statement that "less is more" are each indications of an awareness in the design world that our future should be oriented toward minimization. The works of these men and innumerable other designers are demonstrations of what such minimization can bring about. Through the use of a complex and subtle geometry, a Fuller geodesic dome encloses a maximum of space with a minimum of material. A typical building of Mies van der Rohe's design—less technically sophisticated than a Fuller dome—perhaps involves an even greater simplification of concept, reducing complexity of form and providing a functioning structure of minimal substance, but maximal aesthetic order. In each case, though, concept and information take precedence over the kind of accretion of material and mechanism that is typical of the thoughtless products of modern technological society. In a way, the two men represent an understanding of two contrasting aspects of the same future direction. Fuller is deductive, scientific, mathematical and technical and is prepared to offer an extensive verbal rationale for his proposals. Mies, in contrast, is intuitive, aesthetic, cryptic or silent and leaves us to seek out his meanings for ourselves. These two directions, logical and intuitive, scientific and aesthetic, both place maximum emphasis on concept and ideal, leading to minimalism in physical realization.

As a process, human life is physical, but the experience of human life is conceptual. Our sense of experience is always in the mind, a matter of intake and the understanding of information collected through the senses. Science is concerned with extracting and organizing the information which reality contains in terms of logic—the laws of physics and the language of mathematics. The arts are concerned with the interpretation of reality and the creation of a new reality through the language of form. Science (and its application through technology) has been dominant in the recent past, concentrating its efforts on making human life easy, comfortable and safe. That task is nearing completion, in terms of capability, if not in realization, so that human life experience can become less and less concerned with subsistence and basic needs. Instead, we can expect our experience of life to concern itself more and more with information that is not directly related to survival. Information, in its aspects of scientific knowledge and artistic form, can be seen as ends in themselves—the dominant material of life experience.

The arts are not significant consumers of materials or of energy. The canvas and paint consumed by all living painters, the stone and metal consumed by all living sculptors in the totality of their lives' work must be a tiny fraction of the tonnage of materials required to build one aircraft carrier. The end products of art are as lasting as posterity chooses to make them and require no fuel or significant maintenance. A violin uses a tiny amount of material (all biologically replaceable) and only a small amount of human energy and labor for its creation. It has a life of at least hundreds of years and is all that is required to perform all of the violin literature ever written. Pencil and paper (and even typewriter and ribbon) which make no great demands on scarce resources, make possible all the literary arts and major aspects of scholarship and scientific research.

Design is concerned with activities that are more likely to be consumers of material and energy, but intelligent design is concentrated on maximizing effectiveness while minimizing consumption. Thoughtless and foolish design of houses and other buildings, of automobiles and other powered products, makes all of these things wasteful and destructive. Intelligent design can usually accomplish the same or better results, with a minimum of negative concomitants. A well-planned city, properly related to its surrounding countryside, will offer vast human advantage, will be infinitely less wasteful of material and energy and less destructive of life experience than the disorganization and chaos that are the norm of modern urban life.

One tends to think of these matters as primarily technical problems that require skillful problem solving through invention and intelligent engineering. These are certainly significant aspects of the needed redesign and reform of the human environment. But the inseparable aspect that we call artistic, that concerns itself with finding forms and creating visible forms to convey meaning, is every bit as important. As technical solutions become more complete, art will assume still greater importance.

Once we are all adequately fed, housed and our physical needs cared for, our experience of life becomes a matter of awareness of *how* these things are accomplished. Our awareness of the experiences generated by knowledge and art transcend mere awareness of basic survival. Since we are destined to live in a life environment that is largely humanly created, we need to make the quality of that environment as satisfying and as meaningful as that of the natural environment. Anything less makes all the cumulative progress of civilization seem of doubtful benefit. To be well fed, comfortable and surrounded by mechanical conveniences in a chaotic, urban, technological world, headed for its own destruction, can never mean real stability or happiness. Only a deep understanding of sound design, and enlightened management of the humanly created environment can transform the unsettled reality of this transitional time into an era of stability and genuine quality.

The nature of this book makes a truly comprehensive bibliography an impossibility. This list is limited to references that are actually mentioned in the text, books that have been particularly influential in development of the ideas set forth here and, in some cases, books suggested for further exploration concerning people and topics touched on in this book.

Alexander, Christopher. *Notes on the Synthesis of Form.* Harvard University Press, 1964.

Alvar Aalto. Verlag für Architektur; Girsberger, 1963.

Arnheim, Rudolph. *Art and Visual Perception.* University of California Press, 1954.

Bacon, Edmund N. *Design of Cities.* Viking Press, 1967.

Banham, Reyner. *Theory and Design in the First Machine Age.* Praeger, 1960

Bill, Max. *Robert Maillart.* Verlag für Architektur, 1949.

Blake, Peter. *Marcel Breuer.* Museum of Modern Art, 1949.

———. *The Master Builders.* Knopf, 1964. Also reprinted in three smaller books: *Le Corbusier, Mies van der Rohe,* and *Frank Lloyd Wright.* Pelican, 1965.

Boesiger, Willy. *Le Corbusier: Oeuvre Complète.* Vols. 1–8. Les Editions d'Architecture Erlenbach-Zurich, 1936–70.

Bush-Brown, Albert. *Louis Sullivan.* Braziller, 1960.

Dexel, Walter. *Hausgerät das nicht Veraltet.* Otto Maier Verlag, 1949–50.

Ferebee, Ann. *History of Design from the Victorian Era to the Present.* Van Nostrand Reinhold, 1970.

Fitch, James Marston. *American Building: The Historical Forces That Shaped It.* Houghton Mifflin, 1966.

Fuller, R. Buckminster. *Utopia or Oblivion.* Bantam Books, 1970.

Fuller, R. Buckminster, and Marks, Robert W. *The Dymaxion World of Buckminster Fuller.* Reinhold, 1960.

Giedion, Sigfried. *Mechanization Takes Command.* Oxford University Press, 1948.

———. *Space, Time and Architecture.* Harvard University Press, 1941.

———. *Walter Gropius.* Reinhold, 1962.

Gropius, Walter. *Scope of Total Architecture.* Harper, 1943.

Gutheim, Frederick. *Alvar Aalto.* Braziller, 1960.

Hall, Edward T. *The Hidden Dimension.* Doubleday, 1966.

Heyer, Paul, *Architects on Architecture.* Walker, 1966.

Hitchcock, Henry-Russell. *Architecture, Nineteenth and Twentieth Centuries.* Penguin, 1958.

———. *In the Nature of Materials: The Works of Frank Lloyd Wright.* Duell, Sloan and Pearce, 1942.

Johnson, Philip C. *Mies van der Rohe.* Museum of Modern Art, 1947.

Kaufmann, Edgar. *What is Modern Design?* Museum of Modern Art, 1950.

Kaufmann, Edgar, and Raeburn, Ben. *Frank Lloyd Wright: Writings and Buildings.* Meridian, 1960.

Kepes, Gyorgy, ed. *The Man Made Object.* Braziller, 1966.

Kouwenhoven, John A. *Made in America.* Doubleday, 1951. Reprinted as *The Arts in Modern American Civilization.* Norton, 1967.

Le Corbusier. *Creation Is a Patient Search.* Praeger, 1965.

———. *Towards a New Architecture.* Architectural Press, 1927; Praeger, 1959.

Lynes, Russell. *The Tastemakers.* Harper, 1949.

McHale, John. *R. Buckminster Fuller.* Braziller, 1962.

McHarg, Ian. *Design with Nature.* Doubleday, 1971.

Moholy-Nagy, L. *Vision in Motion.* Theobald, 1947.

Morrison, Hugh. *Louis Sullivan: Prophet of Modern Architecture.* Norton, 1935.

Mumford, Lewis. *Culture of Cities.* Harcourt Brace, 1938.

———. *Sticks and Stones.* Boni and Liveright, 1924; Dover, 1955.

———. *Technics and Civilization.* Harcourt Brace, 1934.

Naylor, Gillian. *The Bauhaus.* Studio Vista/Dutton, 1968.

Norberg-Schulz, Christian. *Existence, Space and Architecture.* Praeger, 1971.

———. *Intentions in Architecture.* Allen and Unvin, 1963; Massachusetts Institute of Technology Press, 1968.

Noyes, Eliot F. *Organic Design in Home Furnishings.* Museum of Modern Art, 1941.

Oliver, Paul, ed. *Shelter and Society.* Praeger, 1969.

Orwell, George. *1984.* New American Library, 1949.

Overy, Paul. *De Stijl.* Studio Vista/Dutton, 1968.

Ozenfant, Amédée. *Foundations of Modern Art.* Brewer, Warren and Putnam, 1931; Dover, 1952.

Papanek, Victor. *Design for the Real World.* Pantheon, 1972; Bantam, 1973.

Pevsner, Nikolaus. *Pioneers of Modern Design.* Pelican, 1960.

———. *Sources of Modern Architecture and Design.* Praeger, 1968.

Rapoport, Amos. *House Form and Culture.* Prentice-Hall, 1969.

Read, Herbert. *Art and Industry.* Faber and Faber, 1934.

Richards, J. M. *An Introduction to Modern Architecture.* Pelican, 1940.

Schaefer, Herwin. *Nineteenth Century Modern.* Praeger, 1970.

Scientific American. *Cities.* Knopf, 1966.

Scully, Vincent, Jr. *Louis I. Kahn.* Braziller, 1962.

Sharp, Dennis. *Modern Architecture and Expressionism.* Braziller, 1966.

Thompson, D'Arcy. *On Growth and Form.* Cambridge University Press, 1952; abridged edition, 1961.

Toffler, Alvin. *Future Shock.* Random House, 1970.

Tunnard, Christopher. *The City of Man.* Scribners, 1953.

———. *Man-Made America: Chaos or Control?* Yale University Press, 1963.

Venturi, Robert. *Complexity and Contradiction in Architecture.* Museum of Modern Art/Doubleday, 1966.

Vitruvius. *Ten Books on Architecture.* Translation by Morris Hicky Morgan. Harvard University Press, 1914; Dover, 1960.

Von Hertzen, Heikki, and Spreiregen, Paul D. *Building a New Town: Finland's New Garden City, Tapiola.* Massachusetts Institute of Technology Press, 1971.

Whyte, Lancelot Law. *Aspects of Form.* Lund Humphries, 1951.

Winger, Hans. *The Bauhaus.* Massachusetts Institute of Technology Press, 1969.

References to illustrations are italicized
and follow other references.

Art Credits